YOUR PERSONAL
HOROSCOPE
2009

TAURUS

YOUR PERSONAL HOROSCOPE 2009

TAURUS

21st April–21st May

igloo

igloo

This edition published by Igloo Books Ltd,
Cottage Farm, Sywell, Northants NN6 0BJ
www.igloo-books.com

Produced for Igloo Books by W. Foulsham & Co. Ltd,
The Publishing House, Bennetts Close, Cippenham,
Slough, Berkshire SL1 5AP, England

ISBN: 978-1-84817-057-5

This is an abridged version of material
originally published in *Old Moore's Horoscope
and Astral Diary*.

Printed and manufactured in China

CONTENTS

INTRODUCTION

Your Personal Horoscopes have been specifically created to allow you to get the most from astrological patterns and the way they have a bearing on not only your zodiac sign, but nuances within it. Using the diary section of the book you can read about the influences and possibilities of each and every day of the year. It will be possible for you to see when you are likely to be cheerful and happy or those times when your nature is in retreat and you will be more circumspect. The diary will help to give you a feel for the specific 'cycles' of astrology and the way they can subtly change your day-to-day life. For example, when you see the sign ☿, this means that the planet Mercury is retrograde at that time. Retrograde means it appears to be running backwards through the zodiac. Such a happening has a significant effect on communication skills, but this is only one small aspect of how the Personal Horoscope can help you.

With Your Personal Horoscope the story doesn't end with the diary pages. It includes simple ways for you to work out the zodiac sign the Moon occupied at the time of your birth, and what this means for your personality. In addition, if you know the time of day you were born, it is possible to discover your Ascendant, yet another important guide to your personal make-up and potential.

Many readers are interested in relationships and in knowing how well they get on with people of other astrological signs. You might also be interested in the way you appear to very different sorts of individuals. If you are such a person, the section on Venus will be of particular interest. Despite the rapidly changing position of this planet, you can work out your Venus sign, and learn what bearing it will have on your life.

Using Your Personal Horoscope you can travel on one of the most fascinating and rewarding journeys that anyone can take – the journey to a better realisation of self.

THE ESSENCE OF TAURUS

Exploring the Personality of Taurus the Bull

(21ST APRIL – 21ST MAY)

What's in a sign?

Taurus is probably one of the most misunderstood signs of the zodiac. Astrologers from the past described those born under the sign of the Bull as being gentle, artistic, stubborn and refined. All of this is quite true, but there is so much more to Taureans and the only reason it isn't always discussed as much as it should be is because of basic Taurean reserve. Taureans are generally modest, and don't tend to assert themselves in a direct sense, unless in self-defence. As a result the sign is often sidelined, if not ignored.

You know what you want from life and are quite willing to work long and hard to get it. However, Taurus is also a great lover of luxury, so when circumstances permit you can be slow, ponderous and even lax. If there is a paradox here it is merely typical of Venus-ruled Taurus. On differing occasions you can be chatty or quiet, bold or timorous, smart or scruffy. It all depends on your commitment to a situation. When you are inspired there is nobody powerful enough to hold you back and when you are passionate you have the proclivities of a Casanova!

There are aspects of your nature that seldom change. For example, you are almost always friendly and approachable, and invariably have a sense of what feels and looks just right. You are capable and can work with your hands as well as your brain. You don't particularly care for dirt or squalid surroundings, preferring cleanliness, and you certainly don't take kindly to abject poverty. Most Taureans prefer the country to the coast, find loving relationships easy to deal with and are quite committed to home and family.

Whilst variety is the spice of life to many zodiac signs this is not necessarily the case for Taurus. Many people born under the sign of the Bull remain happy to occupy a specific position for years on end.

It has been suggested, with more than a grain of truth, that the only thing that can get the Bull moving on occasions is a strategically placed bomb. What matters most, and which shows regularly in your dealings with the world at large, is your innate kindness and your desire to help others.

Taurus resources

The best word to describe Taurean subjects who are working to the best of their ability would be 'practical'. Nebulous situations, where you have to spend long hours thinking things through in a subconscious manner, don't suit you half as much as practical tasks, no matter how complex these might be. If you were to find yourself cast up on a desert island you would have all the necessities of life sorted out in a flash. This is not to suggest that you always recognise this potential in yourself. The problem here is that a very definite lack of self-belief is inclined to make you think that almost anyone else in the world has the edge when it comes to talent.

Another of your greatest resources is your creative potential. You always have the knack of knowing what looks and feels just right. This is as true when it comes to decorating your home as it is regarding matters out there in the big, wide world. If this skill could be allied to confidence on a regular basis, there would be little or nothing to stop you. You may well possess specific skills which others definitely don't have, and you get on best when these are really needed.

Taureans don't mind dealing with routine matters and you have a good administrative ability in a number of different fields. With a deeply intuitive streak (when you are willing to recognise it), it isn't usually hard for you to work out how any particular individual would react under given circumstances. Where you fall down on occasions is that you don't always recognise the great advantages that are yours for the taking, and self-belief could hardly be considered the Taurean's greatest virtue.

Taurus people are good at making lists, even if these are of the mental variety. Your natural warmth makes it possible for you to find friends where others would not, and the sort of advice that you offer is considered and sensible. People feel they can rely on you, a fact that could prove to be one of the most important of your resources. There is nothing at all wrong with using this ability to feather your own nest, particularly since you are not the sort of person who would willingly stand on those around you in order to get where you want to go.

Beneath the surface

To say that you are deep would be a definite understatement. Only you know how far down into the basement some of your considerations and emotions actually go. Because you exhibit a generally practical face to the world at large the true scope of the Taurean mind remains something of a mystery to those around you. Certainly you seem to be uncomplicated and even a little superficial at times, though nothing could be further from the truth. Very little happens to you that fails to be filed away in some recess or other of that great interior that is your mind's library. It may be because of this that Taurus is well known for being able to bear a grudge for a long time. However, what is sometimes forgotten is that you never let a kindness from someone else go without reward, even though it may take you a very long time to find a way to say thank you.

Affairs of the heart are of special importance to you and ties of the romantic kind go as deep as any emotion. Once you love you tend to do so quite unconditionally. It takes months or years of upsets to shake your faith in love, and it's a fact that even in these days of marital splits, Taureans are far more likely than most signs of the zodiac to remain hitched. The simple fact is that you believe in loyalty, absolutely and irrevocably. The thought of letting anyone down once you have given your word is almost unthinkable and if such a situation does occur there are almost always quite definite mitigating factors.

Rules and regulations are easy for you to deal with because you have a natural tendency to order. You are also fairly good at dealing with routines and probably have your own life well sorted out as a result. A word of caution is necessary only when this internal need for order extends too much into your external life. Taureans can be fanatical about having a tidy house or for making things work out exactly as they would wish in a work sense. These tendencies start within the recesses of your own, often closed, mind. The way forward here is to throw open the doors and windows now and again and to let those around you know how you function internally. It isn't easy, because you are quite a closed book at heart. However the exercise is well worthwhile and the results can be quite breathtaking.

Making the best of yourself

Anyone who wants to work to the best of their ability first needs a good deal of self-knowledge. In your case this means recognising just what you are capable of doing and then concentrating in these directions. Of course it's only human nature to be all the things we are not, but this tendency runs deeper in you than it does in the majority of individuals. Use your natural kindness to the full and ally this to your practical ability to get things done. Sorting things out is easy for you, so easy in fact that you sometimes fail to realise that not everyone has these skills to the same extent.

Confidence definitely seems to be evident in the way you deal with the world at large. Of course you know that this often isn't the case, but that doesn't matter. It's the way the world at large views you that counts, so keep moving forward, even on those occasions when you are shaking inside. Use your naturally creative skills to the full and cultivate that innate sense of order in ways that benefit you and the world at a very practical level.

Avoid the tendency to be stubborn by convincing yourself that so many things 'simply don't matter'. An inability to move, simply because you feel annoyed or aggrieved, is certainly going to be more of a hindrance than a help – though there are occasions when, like all facets of nature, it's essential. Cultivate the more cheerful qualities that are endemic to your nature and be prepared to mix freely with as many different sorts of people as you possibly can. Be willing to take on new responsibilities because the more you are able to do so, the greater is your natural sense of self-worth. Stitching all these qualities together and using them to your own advantage isn't always easy, but pays handsomely in the end.

The impressions you give

This is a very interesting section as far as the sign of Taurus is concerned. The reason is very simply that you fail on so many occasions to betray the sheer depth of your own Earth-sign nature. That doesn't mean to say that you come across badly to others. On the contrary, you are probably a very popular person, except with those people who mistreat or cheat others. You have a great sense of what is right, and don't tend to deviate from a point of view once you've come to terms with it.

The world sees you as capable, cheerful and generally active, though with a tendency to be sluggish and lethargic on occasions. Perhaps Taurus needs to explain itself more because even when you are not at your most vibrant best there are invariably reasons. You can be quite secretive, though only usually about yourself. This can make life with the Taurean something of a guessing game on occasions. Certainly you appear to be much more fixed in your attitude than might often be the case. Why should this be so? It's mainly because you do have extremely definite ideas about specific matters, and since you sometimes display these it's natural that others pigeon-hole you as a very 'definite' sort. Actually this is far from being the whole truth but, once again, if you don't explain yourself, others can be left in the dark.

You almost certainly are not short of friends. People recognise that you are friendly, tolerant and extremely supportive. You give the impression of being very trustworthy and people know that they can rely on you to act in a specific manner. If this appears to make you somewhat predictable it doesn't really matter because you are deeply loved, and that's what counts. One fact is almost certain – the world has a greater regard for you in a general sense than you have for yourself.

The way forward

The ideal life for the Taurus subject seems to be one that is settled and happy, with not too much upheaval and plenty of order. Whether or not this truly turns out to be the case depends on a number of factors. For starters, even those born under the sign of the Bull have a boredom threshold. This means that having to respond to change and diversity probably does you more good than you might at first think. At the same time you won't know exactly what you are capable of doing unless you really stretch yourself, and that's something that you are not always willing to do.

You do function best from within loving relationships, and although you can be very passionate, once you have given your heart you don't tend to change your mind readily. Personal and domestic contentment are worth a great deal to you because they represent the platform upon which you build the rest of your life. You don't make a good itinerant and probably won't indulge in travel for its own sake. Of course it does you good to get around, since anything that broadens your horizons has got to be an advantage, but you'll probably always maintain a solid home base and relish the prospect of coming back to it as frequently as possible.

Most Taureans are family people. You can be a capable parent, though tend to be a little more authoritarian than some types. Keeping an ordered sort of life is at the base of your psychology, so that even when you are young and less tidy-minded there is always a basic desire for self-discipline. This often extends to your work, where you are extremely capable and can quite easily work under your own supervision. You recognise the beautiful in all spheres of life and tend to gravitate towards clean and sanitary surroundings.

In matters of health you tend to be fairly robust, though you can suffer somewhat with headaches, often brought about as a result of a stiff neck and stress. This latter is what you should avoid as much as possible. Saying what you feel, and listening carefully to the responses, is definitely of great importance. The more you learn, the wiser you become. This makes you the natural resort of others when they need help and advice. If you try not to underestimate your own abilities, you can rise as far in life as the world at large thinks you are capable of doing. At the end of the day it is important to recognise your popularity. In all probability your friends have a much higher opinion of you than the one you cultivate for yourself.

TAURUS ON THE CUSP

Astrological profiles are altered for those people born at either the beginning or the end of a zodiac sign, or, more properly, on the cusps of a sign. In the case of Taurus this would be on the 21st of April and for two or three days after, and similarly at the end of the sign, probably from the 18th to the 21st of May.

The Aries Cusp – April 21st to April 24th

Although you have all the refinement, breeding and creative flair of the true Taurean, you are definitely more of a go-getter. Knowing what you want from life there is a slight possibility that you might be accused of being bossy and sometimes this slightly hurts your Taurean sensitivity. You have plenty of energy to get through the things that you see as being important but it is quite possible that those around you don't always see things in the same light, and this can be annoying to you. Like the typical Taurean you have great reserves of energy and can work long and hard towards any particular objective although, because Aries is also in attendance, you may push yourself slightly harder than is strictly necessary. Your temper is variable and you may not always display the typical Taurean patience with those around you.

It is possible for Taurus to 'wait in the wings' deliberately and therefore to lose out on some of the most important potential gains as a result. In your case, this is much less likely. You don't worry too much about speaking your mind. You are loving and kind, but even family members know that they will only be able to push you so far. At work, you are capable and have executive ability. Like the Taurean you don't really care for getting your hands dirty, but if needs must you can pitch in with the best of them and enjoy a challenge. You don't worry as much as some of your Taurean friends do, but all the same you regularly expect too much of your nervous system and need frequent periods of rest.

Try not to impose your will on those around you and be content to allow things to happen on their own sometimes. This might not be an easy thing for the Aries-cusp Taurean but it's one of the sure ways to success. Confidence isn't lacking and neither is basic patience, but they do have to be encouraged and nurtured.

The Gemini Cusp – May 18th to May 21st

Oh, what a happy person you are – and how much the world loves you for it! This is definitely the more potentially fortunate of the two Taurean cusps, or at least that is how the majority of the people who know you would view it. The fact is that you are bright and breezy, easygoing and sometimes fickle on occasions, but supporting these trends is a patient, generally contented attitude to life that is both refreshing and inspiring. Getting others on your side is not hard and you have plenty of energy when it is needed the most. All the same you are quite capable of dozing in the sun occasionally and probably put far less stress on your nervous system than either Taurus or Gemini when taken alone.

You don't care too much for routines and you love variety, but yet you retain the creative and artistic qualities that come with the sign of the Bull. You work well and with confidence, but would be very likely to change direction in your career at some stage in your life and are not half so tied to routine as is usually the case for Taurus. With a friendly, and even a passionate, approach to matters of the heart you are an attentive lover and a fond parent. Most people know what you really are because you are only too willing to show them. Working out the true motivations that lurk within your soul is part of your personal search to know 'self' and is extremely important.

All in all, you have exactly what it takes to get on in life and a sense of joy and fun that makes you good to know. Patience balances your need to 'get going', whilst your mischievous streak lightens the load of the sign of Taurus which can, on occasions, take itself rather more seriously than it should.

There are many ways of coping with the requirements of life and, at one time or another, it is likely that you will try them all out. But above and beyond your need to experiment you know what is most important to you and that will always be your ultimate goal. What matters the most is your smile, which is enduring and even alluring.

TAURUS AND ITS ASCENDANTS

The nature of every individual on the planet is composed of the rich variety of zodiac signs and planetary positions that were present at the time of their birth. Your Sun sign, which in your case is Taurus, is one of the many factors when it comes to assessing the unique person you are. Probably the most important consideration, other than your Sun sign, is to establish the zodiac sign that was rising over the eastern horizon at the time that you were born. This is your Ascending or Rising sign. Most popular astrology fails to take account of the Ascendant, and yet its importance remains with you from the very moment of your birth, through every day of your life. The Ascendant is evident in the way you approach the world, and so, when meeting a person for the first time, it is this astrological influence that you are most likely to notice first. Our Ascending sign essentially represents what we appear to be, while the Sun sign is what we feel inside ourselves.

The Ascendant also has the potential for modifying our overall nature. For example, if you were born at a time of day when Taurus was passing over the eastern horizon (this would be around the time of dawn) then you would be classed as a double Taurus. As such, you would typify this zodiac sign, both internally and in your dealings with others. However, if your Ascendant sign turned out to be a Fire sign, such as Leo, there would be a profound alteration of nature, away from the expected qualities of Taurus.

One of the reasons why popular astrology often ignores the Ascendant is that it has always been rather difficult to establish. We have found a way to make this possible by devising an easy-to-use table, which you will find on page 157 of this book. Using this, you can establish your Ascendant sign at a glance. You will need to know your rough time of birth, then it is simply a case of following the instructions.

For those readers who have no idea of their time of birth it might be worth allowing a good friend, or perhaps your partner, to read through the section that follows this introduction. Someone who deals with you on a regular basis may easily discover your Ascending sign, even though you could have some difficulty establishing it for yourself. A good understanding of this component of your nature is essential if you want to be aware of that 'other person' who is responsible for the way you make contact with the world at large. Your Sun sign, Ascendant sign, and the

17

other pointers in this book will, together, allow you a far better understanding of what makes you tick as an individual. Peeling back the different layers of your astrological make-up can be an enlightening experience, and the Ascendant may represent one of the most important layers of all.

Taurus with Taurus Ascendant

The world would see you as being fairly typical of the sign of Taurus, so you are careful, sensitive, well bred and, if other astrological trends agree, very creative. Nothing pleases you more than a tidy environment to live in and a peaceful life. You probably believe that there is a place for everything and will do your best to keep it all where it should be. It's a pity that this sometimes includes people, and you are certain to get rather irritated if they don't behave in the way that you would expect. Despite this, you are generally understanding and are very capable of giving and receiving affection.

Not everyone knows the real you, however, and it is sometimes difficult to tell the world those most personal details that can be locked deep inside. At an emotional level you tend to idealise love somewhat, though if anything this presents itself to the world as a slight 'coldness' on occasions. This is far from the truth, but your tidy mind demands that even the most intimate processes are subjected to the same sense of order with which you view the world at large. Unlike many sign combinations, you don't really rely on the help and support of others because you are more than capable yourself. In the main you live a happy life and have the ability to pass on this trait to those you care for.

Taurus with Gemini Ascendant

This is a generally happy combination which finds you better able to externalise the cultured and creative qualities which are inherent in your Taurean nature. You love to be around interesting and stimulating people and tend to be much more talkative than the typical Taurean is expected to be. The reason why Gemini helps here is because it lightens the load somewhat. Taurus is not the most introspective sign of the zodiac, but it does have that quality, and a good dose of Gemini allows you to speak your mind more freely and, as a result, to know yourself better too.

Although your mind tends to be fairly logical, you also enjoy flashes of insight that can cause you to behave in a less rational way from time to time. This is probably no bad thing because life will never be boring with you around. You try to convince yourself that you take on board all the many and varied opinions that come back at you from others, though there is a slight danger of intellectual snobbery if the responses you get are not the expected ones. You particularly like clean houses, funny people and probably fast cars. Financial rewards can come thick and fast to the Gemini-Ascendant Taurean when the logical but inspirational mind is harnessed to practical matters.

Taurus with Cancer Ascendant

Your main aim in life seems to be to look after everyone and everything that you come across. From your deepest and most enduring human love, right down to the birds in the park, you really do care and you show that natural affection in a thousand different ways. Your nature is sensitive and you are easily moved to tears, though this does not prevent you from pitching in and doing practical things to assist at just about any level. There is a danger that you could stifle those same people whom you set out to assist, and people with this zodiac combination are often unwilling, or unable, to allow their children to grow and leave the nest. More time spent considering what suits you would be no bad thing, but the problem is that you find it almost impossible to imagine any situation that doesn't involve your most basic need, which is to nurture.

You appear not to possess a selfish streak, though it sometimes turns out that, in being certain that you understand the needs and wants of the world, you are nevertheless treading on their toes. This eventual realisation can be very painful, but it isn't a stick with which you should beat yourself because at heart you are one of the kindest people imaginable. Your sense of fair play means that you are a quiet social reformer at heart.

Taurus with Leo Ascendant

Oh dear, this can be rather a hedonistic combination. The trouble is that Taurus tends to have a great sense of what looks and feels right, whilst Leo, being a Cat, is inclined to preen itself on almost any occasion. The combination tends towards self-love, which is all too likely for someone who is perfect. But don't be too dispirited about these facts because there is a great deal going for you in other ways. For a start you have one of the warmest hearts to be found anywhere and you are so brave that others marvel at the courage you display. The mountains that you climb may not be of the large, rocky sort, but you manage to find plenty of pinnacles to scale all the same, and you invariably get to the top.

Routines might bore you a little more than would be the case with Taurus alone, but you don't mind being alone. Why should you? You are probably the nicest person you know! Thus if you were ever to be cast up on a deserted island you would people the place all on your own, and there would never be any crime, untidiness or arguments. Problems only arise when other people are involved. However, in social settings you are charming, good to know and full of ideas that really have legs. You preserve your youth well into middle age, but at base you can tend to worry more than is good for you.

Taurus with Virgo Ascendant

This combination tends to amplify the Taurean qualities that you naturally possess and this is the case because both Taurus and Virgo are Earth signs. However, there are certain factors related to Virgo that show themselves very differently than the sign's cousin Taurus. Virgo is more fussy, nervy and and pedantic than Taurus and all of these qualities are going to show up in your nature at one level or another. On the plus side, you might be slightly less concerned about having a perfect home and a perfect family, and your interest in life appears at a more direct level than that of the true Taurean. You care very much about your home and family and are very loyal to your friends. It's true that you sometimes tend to try and take them over, and you can also show a marked tendency to dominate, but your heart is in the right place, and most people recognise that your caring is genuine.

One problem is that there are very few shades of grey in your life, which is certainly not the case for other zodiac sign combinations. Living your life in the way that you do, there isn't much room for compromise, and this fact alone can prove to be something of a problem where relationships are concerned. In a personal sense you need a partner who is willing to be organised and one who relies heavily on your judgements, which don't change very often.

Taurus with Libra Ascendant

A fortunate combination in many ways, this is a double Venus rulership, since both Taurus and Libra are heavily reliant on the planet of love. You are social, amiable and a natural diplomat, anxious to please and ready to care for just about anyone who shows interest in you. You hate disorder, which means that there is a place for everything and everything in its place. This can throw up the odd paradox, however, since being half Libran you cannot always work out where that place ought to be! You deal with life in a humorous way and are quite capable of seeing the absurd in yourself, as well as in others. Your heart is no bigger than that of the dyed-in-the-wool Taurean, but it sits rather closer to the surface and so others recognise it more.

On those occasions when you know you are standing on firm ground you can show great confidence, even if you have to be ready to change some of your opinions at the drop of a hat. When this happens you can be quite at odds with yourself, because Taurus doesn't take very many U-turns, whereas Libra does. Don't expect to know yourself too well, and keep looking for the funny side of things, because it is within humour that you forge the sort of life that suits you best.

Taurus with Scorpio Ascendant

The first, last and most important piece of advice for you is not to take yourself, or anyone else, too seriously. This might be rather a tall order because Scorpio intensifies the deeper qualities of Taurus and can make you rather lacking in the sense of humour that we all need to live our lives in this most imperfect of worlds. You are naturally sensuous by nature. This shows itself in a host of ways. In all probability you can spend hours in the bath, love to treat yourself to good food and drink and take your greatest pleasure in neat and orderly surroundings. On occasions this can alienate you from those who live in the same house, because other people do need to use the bathroom from time to time, and they cannot remain tidy indefinitely.

You tend to worry a great deal about things which are really not very important, but don't take this statement too seriously or you will begin to worry about this, too! You often need to lighten up and should always do your best to tell yourself that most things are not half so important as they seem to be. Be careful over the selection of a life partner and if possible choose someone who is naturally funny and who does not take life anywhere near as seriously as you are inclined to do. At work you are more than capable and in all probability everyone relies heavily on your wise judgements.

Taurus with Sagittarius Ascendant

A dual nature is evident here, and if it doesn't serve to confuse you, it will certainly be a cause of concern to many of the people with whom you share your life. You like to have a good time and are a natural party-goer. On such occasions you are accommodating, chatty and good to know. But contrast this with the quieter side of Taurus, which is directly opposed to your Sagittarian qualities. The opposition of forces is easy for you to deal with because you inhabit your own body and mind all the time, but it's far less easy for friends and relatives to understand. So on those occasions when you decide that, socially speaking, enough is enough, you may have trouble explaining this to the twelve people who are waiting outside your door with party hats and whoopee cushions.

Confidence to do almost anything is not far from the forefront of your mind and you readily embark on adventures that would have some types flapping about in horror. Here again, it is important to realise that we are not all built the same way and that gentle coaxing is sometimes necessary to bring others round to your point of view. If you really have a fault it could be that you are so busy being your own, rather less than predictable self, that you fail to take the rest of the world into account.

Taurus with Capricorn Ascendant

It might appear on the surface that you are not the most interesting person in the world. This is a pity, for you have an active though very logical mind, so logical in some instances that you would have a great deal in common with Mr Spock. This is the thorn in your flesh, or rather the flesh of everyone else, since you are probably quite happy being exactly what you are. You can think things through in a clear and very practical way and end up taking decisions that are balanced, eminently sensible, but, on occasions, rather dull.

Actually there is a fun machine somewhere deep within that Earth-sign nature and those who know you the best will recognise the fact. Often this combination is attended by a deep and biting sense of humour, but it's of the sort that less intelligent and considered types would find rather difficult to recognise. It is likely that you have no lack of confidence in your own judgement and you have all the attributes necessary to do very well on the financial front. Slow and steady progress is your way and you need to be quite certain before you commit yourself to any new venture. This is a zodiac combination that can soak up years of stress and numerous difficulties, yet still come out on top. Nothing holds you back for long and you tend to be very brave.

Taurus with Aquarius Ascendant

There is nothing that you fail to think about deeply and with great intensity. You are wise, honest and very scientific in your approach to life. Routines are necessary in life, but you have most of them sorted out well in advance and so always have time to look at the next interesting fact. If you don't spend all your time watching documentaries on the television set, you make a good friend and love to socialise. Most of the great discoveries of the world were probably made by people with this sort of astrological combination, though your nature is rather 'odd' on occasions and so can be rather difficult for others to understand.

You may be most surprised when others tell you that you are eccentric, but you don't really mind too much because for half of the time you are not inhabiting the same world as the rest of us. Because you can be delightfully dotty you are probably much loved and cherished by your friends, of which there are likely to be many. Family members probably adore you too and you can be guaranteed to entertain anyone with whom you come into contact. The only fly in the ointment is that you sometimes lose track of reality, whatever that might be, and fly high in your own atmosphere of rarefied possibilities.

Taurus with Pisces Ascendant

You are clearly a very sensitive type of person and that sometimes makes it rather difficult for others to know how they might best approach you. Private and deep, you are nevertheless socially inclined on many occasions. However, because your nature is bottomless it is possible that some types would actually accuse you of being shallow. How can this come about? Well, it's simple really. The fact is that you rarely show anyone what is going on in the deepest recesses of your mind and so your responses can appear to be trite or even ill-considered. This is far from the truth, as those who are allowed into the 'inner sanctum' would readily admit. You are something of a sensualist, and relish staying in bed late and simply pleasing yourself for days on end. However, you are a Taurean at heart so you desire a tidy environment in which to live your usually long life.

You are able to deal with the routine aspects of life quite well and can be a capable worker once you are up and firing on all cylinders. It is very important that you maintain an interest in what you are doing because the recesses of your dreamy mind can sometimes appear to be infinitely more attractive. Your imagination is second to none and this fact can often be turned to your advantage.

Taurus with Aries Ascendant

This is a steady combination, so much so that even experienced astrologers would be unlikely to recognise that the Aries quality is present at all, unless of course they came to know you very well. Your approach to life tends to be slow and considered and there is a great danger that you could suppress those feelings that others of your kind would be only too willing to verbalise. To compensate, you are deeply creative and will think matters through much more readily than more dominant Aries types would be inclined to do. In your dealings with the world, you are, nevertheless, somewhat locked inside yourself and can struggle to achieve the level of communication that you so desperately need. Frustration might follow, were it not for the fact that you possess a quiet determination that, to those in the know, is the clearest window through to your Taurean soul.

The care for others is strong and you certainly demonstrate this at all levels. The fact is that you live a great percentage of your life in service to the people you take to, whilst at the same time being able to shut the door firmly in the face of people who irritate or anger you. You are deeply motivated towards family relationships.

THE MOON AND THE PART IT PLAYS IN YOUR LIFE

In astrology the Moon is probably the single most important heavenly body after the Sun. Its unique position, as partner to the Earth on its journey around the solar system, means that the Moon appears to pass through the signs of the zodiac extremely quickly. The zodiac position of the Moon at the time of your birth plays a great part in personal character and is especially significant in the build-up of your emotional nature.

Your Own Moon Sign

Discovering the position of the Moon at the time of your birth has always been notoriously difficult because tracking the complex zodiac positions of the Moon is not easy. This process has been reduced to three simple stages with our Lunar Tables. A breakdown of the Moon's zodiac positions can be found from page 35 onwards, so that once you know what your Moon Sign is, you can see what part this plays in the overall build-up of your personal character.

If you follow the instructions on the next page you will soon be able to work out exactly what zodiac sign the Moon occupied on the day that you were born and you can then go on to compare the reading for this position with those of your Sun sign and your Ascendant. It is partly the comparison between these three important positions that goes towards making you the unique individual you are.

HOW TO DISCOVER YOUR MOON SIGN

This is a three-stage process. You may need a pen and a piece of paper but if you follow the instructions below the process should only take a minute or so.

STAGE 1 First of all you need to know the Moon Age at the time of your birth. If you look at Moon Table 1, on page 33, you will find all the years between 1911 and 2009 down the left side. Find the year of your birth and then trace across to the right to the month of your birth. Where the two intersect you will find a number. This is the date of the New Moon in the month that you were born. You now need to count forward the number of days between the New Moon and your own birthday. For example, if the New Moon in the month of your birth was shown as being the 6th and you were born on the 20th, your Moon Age Day would be 14. If the New Moon in the month of your birth came after your birthday, you need to count forward from the New Moon in the previous month. If you were born in a Leap Year, remember to count the 29th February. You can tell if your birth year was a Leap Year if the last two digits can be divided by four. Whatever the result, jot this number down so that you do not forget it.

STAGE 2 Take a look at Moon Table 2 on page 34. Down the left hand column look for the date of your birth. Now trace across to the month of your birth. Where the two meet you will find a letter. Copy this letter down alongside your Moon Age Day.

STAGE 3 Moon Table 3 on page 34 will supply you with the zodiac sign the Moon occupied on the day of your birth. Look for your Moon Age Day down the left hand column and then for the letter you found in Stage 2. Where the two converge you will find a zodiac sign and this is the sign occupied by the Moon on the day that you were born.

Your Zodiac Moon Sign Explained

You will find a profile of all zodiac Moon Signs on pages 35 to 38, showing in yet another way how astrology helps to make you into the individual that you are. In each daily entry of the Astral Diary you can find the zodiac position of the Moon for every day of the year. This also allows you to discover your lunar birthdays. Since the Moon passes through all the signs of the zodiac in about a month, you can expect something like twelve lunar birthdays each year. At these times you are likely to be emotionally steady and able to make the sort of decisions that have real, lasting value.

MOON TABLE 1

YEAR	MAR	APR	MAY	YEAR	MAR	APR	MAY	YEAR	MAR	APR	MAY
1911	30	28	28	1944	24	22	22	1977	19	18	18
1912	19	18	17	1945	14	12	11	1978	9	7	7
1913	7	6	5	1946	3	2	1/30	1979	27	26	26
1914	26	24	24	1947	21	20	19	1980	16	15	14
1915	15	13	13	1948	11	9	9	1981	6	4	4
1916	5	3	2	1949	29	28	27	1982	24	23	21
1917	23	22	20	1950	18	17	17	1983	14	13	12
1918	12	11	10	1951	7	6	6	1984	2	1	1/30
1919	2/31	30	29	1952	25	24	23	1985	21	20	19
1920	20	18	18	1953	15	13	13	1986	10	9	8
1921	9	8	7	1954	5	3	2	1987	29	28	27
1922	28	27	26	1955	24	22	21	1988	18	16	15
1923	17	16	15	1956	12	11	10	1989	7	6	5
1924	5	4	3	1957	1/31	29	29	1990	26	25	24
1925	24	23	22	1958	20	19	18	1991	15	13	13
1926	14	12	11	1959	9	8	7	1992	4	3	2
1927	3	2	1/30	1960	27	26	26	1993	24	22	21
1928	21	20	19	1961	16	15	14	1994	12	11	10
1929	11	9	9	1962	6	5	4	1995	30	29	29
1930	30	28	28	1963	25	23	23	1996	19	18	18
1931	19	18	17	1964	14	12	11	1997	9	7	6
1932	7	6	5	1965	2	1	1/30	1998	27	26	25
1933	26	24	24	1966	21	20	19	1999	17	16	15
1934	15	13	13	1967	10	9	8	2000	6	4	4
1935	5	3	2	1968	29	28	27	2001	24	23	22
1936	23	21	20	1969	18	16	15	2002	13	12	10
1937	13	12	10	1970	7	6	6	2003	2	1	1/30
1938	2/31	30	29	1971	26	25	24	2004	21	19	18
1939	20	19	19	1972	15	13	13	2005	10	8	8
1940	9	7	7	1973	5	3	2	2006	29	27	27
1941	27	26	26	1974	24	22	21	2007	18	17	15
1942	16	15	15	1975	12	11	11	2008	7	6	5
1943	6	4	4	1976	30	29	29	2009	26	25	24

TABLE 2

MOON TABLE 3

DAY	APR	MAY	M/D	J	K	L	M	N	O	P
1	J	M	0	AR	TA	TA	TA	GE	GE	GE
2	J	M	1	TA	TA	TA	GE	GE	GE	CA
3	J	M	2	TA	TA	GE	GE	GE	CA	CA
4	J	M	3	TA	GE	GE	GE	CA	CA	CA
5	J	M	4	GE	GE	GE	CA	CA	CA	LE
6	J	M	5	GE	CA	CA	CA	LE	LE	LE
7	J	M	6	CA	CA	CA	LE	LE	LE	VI
8	J	M	7	CA	CA	LE	LE	LE	VI	VI
9	J	M	8	CA	LE	LE	LE	VI	VI	VI
10	J	M	9	LE	LE	VI	VI	VI	LI	LI
11	K	M	10	LE	VI	VI	VI	LI	LI	LI
12	K	N	11	VI	VI	VI	LI	LI	SC	SC
13	K	N	12	VI	VI	LI	LI	LI	SC	SC
14	K	N	13	VI	LI	LI	LI	SC	SC	SC
15	K	N	14	LI	LI	LI	SC	SC	SA	SA
16	K	N	15	LI	SC	SC	SC	SA	SA	SA
17	K	N	16	SC	SC	SC	SA	SA	SA	CP
18	K	N	17	SC	SC	SA	SA	SA	CP	CP
19	K	N	18	SC	SA	SA	SA	CP	CP	CP
20	K	N	19	SA	SA	SA	CP	CP	CP	AQ
21	L	N	20	SA	CP	CP	CP	AQ	AQ	AQ
22	L	O	21	CP	CP	CP	AQ	AQ	AQ	PI
23	L	O	22	CP	CP	AQ	AQ	AQ	PI	PI
24	L	O	23	CP	AQ	AQ	AQ	PI	PI	PI
25	L	O	24	AQ	AQ	AQ	PI	PI	PI	AR
26	L	O	25	AQ	PI	PI	PI	AR	AR	AR
27	L	O	26	PI	PI	PI	AR	AR	AR	TA
28	L	O	27	PI	PI	AR	AR	AR	TA	TA
29	L	O	28	PI	AR	AR	AR	TA	TA	TA
30	L	O	29	AR	AR	AR	TA	TA	TA	GE
31	–	O								

AR = Aries, TA = Taurus, GE = Gemini, CA = Cancer, LE = Leo, VI = Virgo, LI = Libra, SC = Scorpio, SA = Sagittarius, CP = Capricorn, AQ = Aquarius, PI = Pisces

MOON SIGNS

Moon in Aries

You have a strong imagination, courage, determination and a desire to do things in your own way and forge your own path through life.

Originality is a key attribute; you are seldom stuck for ideas although your mind is changeable and you could take the time to focus on individual tasks. Often quick-tempered, you take orders from few people and live life at a fast pace. Avoid health problems by taking regular time out for rest and relaxation.

Emotionally, it is important that you talk to those you are closest to and work out your true feelings. Once you discover that people are there to help, there is less necessity for you to do everything yourself.

Moon in Taurus

The Moon in Taurus gives you a courteous and friendly manner, which means you are likely to have many friends.

The good things in life mean a lot to you, as Taurus is an Earth sign that delights in experiences which please the senses. Hence you are probably a lover of good food and drink, which may in turn mean you need to keep an eye on the bathroom scales, especially as looking good is also important to you.

Emotionally you are fairly stable and you stick by your own standards. Taureans do not respond well to change. Intuition also plays an important part in your life.

Moon in Gemini

You have a warm-hearted character, sympathetic and eager to help others. At times reserved, you can also be articulate and chatty: this is part of the paradox of Gemini, which always brings duplicity to the nature. You are interested in current affairs, have a good intellect, and are good company and likely to have many friends. Most of your friends have a high opinion of you and would be ready to defend you should the need arise. However, this is usually unnecessary, as you are quite capable of defending yourself in any verbal confrontation.

Travel is important to your inquisitive mind and you find intellectual stimulus in mixing with people from different cultures. You also gain much from reading, writing and the arts but you do need plenty of rest and relaxation in order to avoid fatigue.

Moon in Cancer

The Moon in Cancer at the time of birth is a fortunate position as Cancer is the Moon's natural home. This means that the qualities of compassion and understanding given by the Moon are especially enhanced in your nature, and you are friendly and sociable and cope well with emotional pressures. You cherish home and family life, and happily do the domestic tasks. Your surroundings are important to you and you hate squalor and filth. You are likely to have a love of music and poetry.

Your basic character, although at times changeable like the Moon itself, depends on symmetry. You aim to make your surroundings comfortable and harmonious, for yourself and those close to you.

Moon in Leo

The best qualities of the Moon and Leo come together to make you warm-hearted, fair, ambitious and self-confident. With good organisational abilities, you invariably rise to a position of responsibility in your chosen career. This is fortunate as you don't enjoy being an 'also-ran' and would rather be an important part of a small organisation than a menial in a large one.

You should be lucky in love, and happy, provided you put in the effort to make a comfortable home for yourself and those close to you. It is likely that you will have a love of pleasure, sport, music and literature. Life brings you many rewards, most of them as a direct result of your own efforts, although you may be luckier than average and ready to make the best of any situation.

Moon in Virgo

You are endowed with good mental abilities and a keen receptive memory, but you are never ostentatious or pretentious. Naturally quite reserved, you still have many friends, especially of the opposite sex. Marital relationships must be discussed carefully and worked at so that they remain harmonious, as personal attachments can be a problem if you do not give them your full attention.

Talented and persevering, you possess artistic qualities and are a good homemaker. Earning your honours through genuine merit, you work long and hard towards your objectives but show little pride in your achievements. Many short journeys will be undertaken in your life.

Moon in Libra

With the Moon in Libra you are naturally popular and make friends easily. People like you, probably more than you realise, you bring fun to a party and are a natural diplomat. For all its good points, Libra is not the most stable of astrological signs and, as a result, your emotions can be a little unstable too. Therefore, although the Moon in Libra is said to be good for love and marriage, your Sun sign and Rising sign will have an important effect on your emotional and loving qualities.

You must remember to relate to others in your decision-making. Co-operation is crucial because Libra represents the 'balance' of life that can only be achieved through harmonious relationships. Conformity is not easy for you because Libra, an Air sign, likes its independence.

Moon in Scorpio

Some people might call you pushy. In fact, all you really want to do is to live life to the full and protect yourself and your family from the pressures of life. Take care to avoid giving the impression of being sarcastic or impulsive and use your energies wisely and constructively.

You have great courage and you invariably achieve your goals by force of personality and sheer effort. You are fond of mystery and are good at predicting the outcome of situations and events. Travel experiences can be beneficial to you.

You may experience problems if you do not take time to examine your motives in a relationship, and also if you allow jealousy, always a feature of Scorpio, to cloud your judgement.

Moon in Sagittarius

The Moon in Sagittarius helps to make you a generous individual with humanitarian qualities and a kind heart. Restlessness may be intrinsic as your mind is seldom still. Perhaps because of this, you have a need for change that could lead you to several major moves during your adult life. You are not afraid to stand your ground when you know your judgement is right, you speak directly and have good intuition.

At work you are quick, efficient and versatile and so you make an ideal employee. You need work to be intellectually demanding and do not enjoy tedious routines.

In relationships, you anger quickly if faced with stupidity or deception, though you are just as quick to forgive and forget. Emotionally, there are times when your heart rules your head.

37

Moon in Capricorn

The Moon in Capricorn makes you popular and likely to come into the public eye in some way. The watery Moon is not entirely comfortable in the Earth sign of Capricorn and this may lead to some difficulties in the early years of life. An initial lack of creative ability and indecision must be overcome before the true qualities of patience and perseverance inherent in Capricorn can show through.

You have good administrative ability and are a capable worker, and if you are careful you can accumulate wealth. But you must be cautious and take professional advice in partnerships, as you are open to deception. You may be interested in social or welfare work, which suit your organisational skills and sympathy for others.

Moon in Aquarius

The Moon in Aquarius makes you an active and agreeable person with a friendly, easy-going nature. Sympathetic to the needs of others, you flourish in a laid-back atmosphere. You are broad-minded, fair and open to suggestion, although sometimes you have an unconventional quality which others can find hard to understand.

You are interested in the strange and curious, and in old articles and places. You enjoy trips to these places and gain much from them. Political, scientific and educational work interests you and you might choose a career in science or technology.

Money-wise, you make gains through innovation and concentration and Lunar Aquarians often tackle more than one job at a time. In love you are kind and honest.

Moon in Pisces

You have a kind, sympathetic nature, somewhat retiring at times, but you always take account of others' feelings and help when you can.

Personal relationships may be problematic, but as life goes on you can learn from your experiences and develop a better understanding of yourself and the world around you.

You have a fondness for travel, appreciate beauty and harmony and hate disorder and strife. You may be fond of literature and would make a good writer or speaker yourself. You have a creative imagination and may come across as an incurable romantic. You have strong intuition, maybe bordering on a mediumistic quality, which sets you apart from the mass. You may not be rich in cash terms, but your personal gifts are worth more than gold.

TAURUS IN LOVE

Discover how compatible you are with people from the same and other signs of the zodiac. Five stars equals a match made in heaven!

Taurus meets Taurus

A certainty for complete success or absolute failure. Taurus has enough self-knowledge to recognise the strengths of a fellow Taurean, so these two can live in harmony. Both will be tidy and live in comfortable surroundings. Two Taureans seldom argue and will be good friends. But something may be lacking – a spark that doesn't ignite. Passion is important and Taurus reflects, rather than creates it. The prognosis is good, but someone must turn the heat up to get things really cooking. Star rating: ****

Taurus meets Gemini

Gemini people can infuriate the generally steady Taurean nature as they are so untidy, which is a complete reversal of the Taurean ethos. At first this won't matter; Mr or Miss Gemini is enchanting, entertaining and very different. But time will tell, and that's why this potential relationship only has two stars. There is hope, however, because Taurus can curb some of the excesses of the Twins, whilst Gemini is capable of preventing the Bull from taking itself too seriously. Star rating: **

Taurus meets Cancer

This pair will have the tidiest house in the street – every stick of furniture in place, and no errant blade of grass daring to spoil the lawn. But things inside the relationship might not be quite so ship-shape as both signs need, but don't offer, encouragement. There's plenty of affection, but few incentives for mutual progress. This might not prevent material success, but an enduring relationship isn't based on money alone. Passion is essential, and both parties need to realise and aim for that. Star rating: **

Taurus meets Leo

Here we find a generally successful pairing, which frequently leads to an enduring relationship. Taurus needs stimulation which Leo is happy to offer, while Leo responds well to the Bull's sense of order. The essence of the relationship is balance, but it may be achieved with wild swings of the scales on the way, so don't expect a quiet life, though this pair will enjoy a reconciliation after an argument! Material success is probable and, as both like children, a family is likely. Star rating: ***

Taurus meets Virgo

This is a difficult basis for a successful relationship, and yet it often works. Both signs are from the Earth element, so have a common-sense approach to life. They have a mutual understanding, and share many interests. Taurus understands and copes well with Virgo's fussy nature, while Virgo revels in the Bull's tidy and artistic qualities. Both sides are committed to achieving lasting material success. There won't be fireworks, and the match may lack a certain 'spiritual' feel, but as that works both ways it may not be a problem. Star rating: *****

Taurus meets Libra

A happy life is important to both these signs and, as they are both ruled by Venus, they share a common understanding, even though they display themselves so differently. Taurus is quieter than Libra, but can be decisive, and that's what counts. Libra is interested in absolutely everything, an infectious quality when seen through Taurean eyes. The slightly flighty qualities of Libra may lead to jealousy from the Bull. Not an argumentative relationship and one that often works well. There could be many changes of address for this pair. Star rating: ****

Taurus meets Scorpio

Scorpio is deep – very deep – which may be a problem, because Taurus doesn't wear its heart on its sleeve either. It might be difficult for this pair to get together, because neither are naturally inclined to make the first move. Taurus stands in awe of the power and intensity of the Scorpio mind, while the Scorpion is interested in the Bull's affable and friendly qualities, so an enduring relationship could be forged if the couple ever get round to talking. Both are lovers of home and family, which will help to cement a relationship. Star rating: **

Taurus meets Sagittarius

On first impression, Taurus may not like Sagittarius, who may seem brash, and even common, when viewed through the Bull's refined eyes. But there is hope of success because the two signs have so much to offer each other. The Archer is enthralled by the Taurean's natural poise and beauty, while Taurus always needs more basic confidence, which is no problem to Sagittarius who has plenty to spare. Both signs love to travel. There are certain to be ups and downs, but that doesn't prevent an interesting, inspiring and even exciting combination. Star rating: ***

Taurus meets Capricorn

If not quite a match made in heaven, this comes close. Both signs are earthy in nature and that is a promising start. Capricorn is very practical and can make a Taurean's dreams come true. Both are tidy, like to know what is going to happen in a day-to-day sense, and are steady and committed. Taurus loves refinement, which Capricorn accepts and even helps to create. A good prognosis for material success rounds off a relationship that could easily stay the course. The only thing missing is a genuine sense of humour. Star rating: *****

Taurus meets Aquarius

In any relationship of which Aquarius is a part, surprises abound. It is difficult for Taurus to understand the soul-searching, adventurous, changeable Aquarian, but on the positive side, the Bull is adaptable and can respond well to a dose of excitement. Aquarians are kind and react well to the same quality coming back at them. Both are friendly, capable of deep affection and basically quite creative. Unfortunately, though, Taurus simply doesn't know what makes Aquarius tick, which could lead to hidden feelings of isolation. Star rating: **

Taurus meets Pisces

No problem here, unless both parties come from the quieter side of their respective signs. Most of the time Taurus and Pisces would live comfortably together, offering mutual support and deep regard. Taurus can offer the personal qualities that Pisces craves, whilst Pisces understands and copes with the Bull's slightly stubborn qualities. Taurus is likely to travel in Piscean company, so there is a potential for wide-ranging experiences and variety which is essential. There will be some misunderstandings, mainly because Pisces is so deep, but that won't prevent their enduring happiness. Star rating: ***

Taurus meets Aries

This match has been known to work very well. Aries brings dynamism and ambition, while Taurus has the patience to see things through logically. Such complementary views work equally well in a relationship or in an office environment. There is mutual respect, but sometimes a lack of total understanding. The romantic needs of each sign are quite different, but both are still fulfilled. Taurus and Aries can live easily in domestic harmony which is very important but, interestingly, Aries may be the loser in battles of will. Star rating: ***

VENUS:
THE PLANET OF LOVE

If you look up at the sky around sunset or sunrise you will often see Venus in close attendance to the Sun. It is arguably one of the most beautiful sights of all and there is little wonder that historically it became associated with the goddess of love. But although Venus does play an important part in the way you view love and in the way others see you romantically, this is only one of the spheres of influence that it enjoys in your overall character.

Venus has a part to play in the more cultured side of your life and has much to do with your appreciation of art, literature, music and general creativity. Even the way you look is responsive to the part of the zodiac that Venus occupied at the start of your life, though this fact is also down to your Sun sign and Ascending sign. If, at the time you were born, Venus occupied one of the more gregarious zodiac signs, you will be more likely to wear your heart on your sleeve, as well as to be more attracted to entertainment, social gatherings and good company. If on the other hand Venus occupied a quiet zodiac sign at the time of your birth, you would tend to be more retiring and less willing to shine in public situations.

It's good to know what part the planet Venus plays in your life, for it can have a great bearing on the way you appear to the rest of the world and since we all have to mix with others, you can learn to make the very best of what Venus has to offer you.

One of the great complications in the past has always been trying to establish exactly what zodiac position Venus enjoyed when you were born, because the planet is notoriously difficult to track. However, we have solved that problem by creating a table that is exclusive to your Sun sign, which you will find on the following page.

Establishing your Venus sign could not be easier. Just look up the year of your birth on the following page and you will see a sign of the zodiac. This was the sign that Venus occupied in the period covered by your sign in that year. If Venus occupied more than one sign during the period, this is indicated by the date on which the sign changed, and the name of the new sign. For instance, if you were born in 1950, Venus was in Pisces until the 5th May, after which time it was in Aries. If you were born before 5th May your Venus sign is Pisces, if you were born on or after 5th May, your Venus sign is Aries. Once you have established the position of Venus at the time of your birth, you can then look in the pages which follow to see how this has a bearing on your life as a whole.

43

1911 GEMINI / 13.5 CANCER
1912 ARIES / 8.5 TAURUS
1913 TAURUS / 30.4 ARIES
1914 TAURUS / 2.5 GEMINI
1915 PISCES / 27.4 ARIES
1916 GEMINI / 6.5 CANCER
1917 TAURUS / 16.5 GEMINI
1918 PISCES / 7.5 ARIES
1919 GEMINI / 13.5 CANCER
1920 ARIES / 7.5 TAURUS
1921 TAURUS / 27.4 ARIES
1922 TAURUS / 2.5 GEMINI
1923 PISCES / 27.4 ARIES
1924 GEMINI / 7.5 CANCER
1925 TAURUS / 16.5 GEMINI
1926 PISCES / 6.5 ARIES
1927 GEMINI / 12.5 CANCER
1928 ARIES / 6.5 TAURUS
1929 TAURUS / 24.4 ARIES
1930 TAURUS / 1.5 GEMINI
1931 PISCES / 26.4 ARIES
1932 GEMINI / 8.5 CANCER
1933 TAURUS / 15.5 GEMINI
1934 PISCES / 6.5 ARIES
1935 GEMINI / 12.5 CANCER
1936 ARIES / 6.5 TAURUS
1937 TAURUS / 21.4 ARIES
1938 TAURUS / 1.5 GEMINI
1939 PISCES / 26.4 ARIES
1940 GEMINI / 9.5 CANCER
1941 TAURUS / 14.5 GEMINI
1942 PISCES / 6.5 ARIES
1943 GEMINI / 11.5 CANCER
1944 ARIES / 6.5 TAURUS
1945 ARIES
1946 TAURUS / 30.4 GEMINI
1947 PISCES / 25.4 ARIES
1948 GEMINI / 9.5 CANCER
1949 TAURUS / 14.5 GEMINI
1950 PISCES / 5.5 ARIES
1951 GEMINI / 11.5 CANCER
1952 ARIES / 5.5 TAURUS
1953 ARIES
1954 TAURUS / 29.4 GEMINI
1955 PISCES / 25.4 ARIES
1956 GEMINI / 10.5 CANCER
1957 TAURUS / 13.5 GEMINI
1958 PISCES / 5.5 ARIES
1959 GEMINI / 10.5 CANCER
1960 ARIES / 4.5 TAURUS

1961 ARIES
1962 TAURUS / 28.4 GEMINI
1963 PISCES / 24.4 ARIES
1964 GEMINI / 11.5 CANCER
1965 TAURUS / 13.5 GEMINI
1966 PISCES / 5.5 ARIES
1967 GEMINI / 10.5 CANCER
1968 ARIES / 4.5 TAURUS
1969 ARIES
1970 TAURUS / 27.4 GEMINI
1971 PISCES / 24.4 ARIES
1972 GEMINI / 12.5 CANCER
1973 TAURUS / 12.5 GEMINI
1974 PISCES / 4.5 ARIES
1975 GEMINI / 9.5 CANCER
1976 ARIES / 3.5 TAURUS
1977 ARIES
1978 TAURUS / 27.4 GEMINI
1979 PISCES / 23.4 ARIES
1980 GEMINI / 13.5 CANCER
1981 TAURUS / 12.5 GEMINI
1982 PISCES / 4.5 ARIES
1983 GEMINI / 9.5 CANCER
1984 ARIES / 3.5 TAURUS
1985 ARIES
1986 TAURUS / 26.4 GEMINI
1987 PISCES / 23.4 ARIES
1988 GEMINI / 15.5 CANCER
1989 TAURUS / 11.5 GEMINI
1990 PISCES / 4.5 ARIES
1991 GEMINI / 8.5 CANCER
1992 ARIES / 2.5 TAURUS
1993 ARIES
1994 TAURUS / 26.4 GEMINI
1995 PISCES / 22.4 ARIES
1996 GEMINI / 15.5 CANCER
1997 TAURUS / 11.5 GEMINI
1998 PISCES / 3.5 ARIES
1999 GEMINI / 8.5 CANCER
2000 ARIES / 2.5 TAURUS
2001 ARIES
2002 TAURUS / 26.4 GEMINI
2003 PISCES / 22.4 ARIES
2004 GEMINI / 15.5 CANCER
2005 TAURUS / 11.5 GEMINI
2006 PISCES / 3.5 ARIES
2007 GEMINI / 8.5 CANCER
2008 ARIES / 2.5 TAURUS
2009 ARIES

VENUS THROUGH
THE ZODIAC SIGNS

Venus in Aries

Amongst other things, the position of Venus in Aries indicates a fondness for travel, music and all creative pursuits. Your nature tends to be affectionate and you would try not to create confusion or difficulty for others if it could be avoided. Many people with this planetary position have a great love of the theatre, and mental stimulation is of the greatest importance. Early romantic attachments are common with Venus in Aries, so it is very important to establish a genuine sense of romantic continuity. Early marriage is not recommended, especially if it is based on sympathy. You may give your heart a little too readily on occasions.

Venus in Taurus

You are capable of very deep feelings and your emotions tend to last for a very long time. This makes you a trusting partner and lover, whose constancy is second to none. In life you are precise and careful and always try to do things the right way. Although this means an ordered life, which you are comfortable with, it can also lead you to be rather too fussy for your own good. Despite your pleasant nature, you are very fixed in your opinions and quite able to speak your mind. Others are attracted to you and historical astrologers always quoted this position of Venus as being very fortunate in terms of marriage. However, if you find yourself involved in a failed relationship, it could take you a long time to trust again.

Venus in Gemini

As with all associations related to Gemini, you tend to be quite versatile, anxious for change and intelligent in your dealings with the world at large. You may gain money from more than one source but you are equally good at spending it. There is an inference here that you are a good communicator, via either the written or the spoken word, and you love to be in the company of interesting people. Always on the look-out for culture, you may also be very fond of music, and love to indulge the curious and cultured side of your nature. In romance you tend to have more than one relationship and could find yourself associated with someone who has previously been a friend or even a distant relative.

Venus in Cancer

You often stay close to home because you are very fond of family and enjoy many of your most treasured moments when you are with those you love. Being naturally sympathetic, you will always do anything you can to support those around you, even people you hardly know at all. This charitable side of your nature is your most noticeable trait and is one of the reasons why others are naturally so fond of you. Being receptive and in some cases even psychic, you can see through to the soul of most of those with whom you come into contact. You may not commence too many romantic attachments but when you do give your heart, it tends to be unconditionally.

Venus in Leo

It must become quickly obvious to almost anyone you meet that you are kind, sympathetic and yet determined enough to stand up for anyone or anything that is truly important to you. Bright and sunny, you warm the world with your natural enthusiasm and would rarely do anything to hurt those around you, or at least not intentionally. In romance you are ardent and sincere, though some may find your style just a little overpowering. Gains come through your contacts with other people and this could be especially true with regard to romance, for love and money often come hand in hand for those who were born with Venus in Leo. People claim to understand you, though you are more complex than you seem.

Venus in Virgo

Your nature could well be fairly quiet no matter what your Sun sign might be, though this fact often manifests itself as an inner peace and would not prevent you from being basically sociable. Some delays and even the odd disappointment in love cannot be ruled out with this planetary position, though it's a fact that you will usually find the happiness you look for in the end. Catapulting yourself into romantic entanglements that you know to be rather ill-advised is not sensible, and it would be better to wait before you committed yourself exclusively to any one person. It is the essence of your nature to serve the world at large and through doing so it is possible that you will attract money at some stage in your life.

Venus in Libra

Venus is very comfortable in Libra and bestows upon those people who have this planetary position a particular sort of kindness that is easy to recognise. This is a very good position for all sorts of friendships and also for romantic attachments that usually bring much joy into your life. Few individuals with Venus in Libra would avoid marriage and since you are capable of great depths of love, it is likely that you will find a contented personal life. You like to mix with people of integrity and intelligence but don't take kindly to scruffy surroundings or work that means getting your hands too dirty. Careful speculation, good business dealings and money through marriage all seem fairly likely.

Venus in Scorpio

You are quite open and tend to spend money quite freely, even on those occasions when you don't have very much. Although your intentions are always good, there are times when you get yourself in to the odd scrape and this can be particularly true when it comes to romance, which you may come to late or from a rather unexpected direction. Certainly you have the power to be happy and to make others contented on the way, but you find the odd stumbling block on your journey through life and it could seem that you have to work harder than those around you. As a result of this, you gain a much deeper understanding of the true value of personal happiness than many people ever do, and are likely to achieve true contentment in the end.

Venus in Sagittarius

You are lighthearted, cheerful and always able to see the funny side of any situation. These facts enhance your popularity, which is especially high with members of the opposite sex. You should never have to look too far to find romantic interest in your life, though it is just possible that you might be too willing to commit yourself before you are certain that the person in question is right for you. Part of the problem here extends to other areas of life too. The fact is that you like variety in everything and so can tire of situations that fail to offer it. All the same, if you choose wisely and learn to understand your restless side, then great happiness can be yours.

Venus in Capricorn

The most notable trait that comes from Venus in this position is that it makes you trustworthy and able to take on all sorts of responsibilities in life. People are instinctively fond of you and love you all the more because you are always ready to help those who are in any form of need. Social and business popularity can be yours and there is a magnetic quality to your nature that is particularly attractive in a romantic sense. Anyone who wants a partner for a lover, a spouse and a good friend too would almost certainly look in your direction. Constancy is the hallmark of your nature and unfaithfulness would go right against the grain. You might sometimes be a little too trusting.

Venus in Aquarius

This location of Venus offers a fondness for travel and a desire to try out something new at every possible opportunity. You are extremely easy to get along with and tend to have many friends from varied backgrounds, classes and inclinations. You like to live a distinct sort of life and gain a great deal from moving about, both in a career sense and with regard to your home. It is not out of the question that you could form a romantic attachment to someone who comes from far away or be attracted to a person of a distinctly artistic and original nature. What you cannot stand is jealousy, for you have friends of both sexes and would want to keep things that way.

Venus in Pisces

The first thing people tend to notice about you is your wonderful, warm smile. Being very charitable by nature you will do anything to help others, even if you don't know them well. Much of your life may be spent sorting out situations for other people, but it is very important to feel that you are living for yourself too. In the main, you remain cheerful, and tend to be quite attractive to members of the opposite sex. Where romantic attachments are concerned, you could be drawn to people who are significantly older or younger than yourself or to someone with a unique career or point of view. It might be best for you to avoid marrying whilst you are still very young.

TAURUS:
2008 DIARY PAGES

October

2008

1 WEDNESDAY ☿ *Moon Age Day 1   Moon Sign Libra*

The first day of October can be active, enterprising and sometimes quite surprising in what it throws into your path. If by the evening some of the drive you have been maintaining starts to diminish, you might decide to slump in front of the television. A quieter spell probably turns out to be no bad thing.

2 THURSDAY ☿ *Moon Age Day 2   Moon Sign Scorpio*

The lunar low is best served by keeping things as simple as you can and life could take on a rather 'so-so' quality for the next couple of days. This is not to say that you fail to make any headway at all, merely that you do better if you tackle one job at once, which is probably not what you have been doing across the last few days.

3 FRIDAY ☿ *Moon Age Day 3   Moon Sign Scorpio*

If there are impediments to your progress at the moment, there may not be very much you can do to remove them. All in all it would be better to avoid taking on too much and to consolidate what you already have. Rest and recuperation are in order, together with spending quiet time in the company of someone who is dear to you.

4 SATURDAY ☿ *Moon Age Day 4   Moon Sign Sagittarius*

Mars remains in your solar sixth house, and from a practical point of view this planetary position allows you to stay on your toes. The lunar low has now gone and you can once again show yourself to be both positive and quite dynamic in your attitude. Stand by to make a few gains you didn't expect – and one or two of them could be financial.

5 SUNDAY ☿ *Moon Age Day 5   Moon Sign Sagittarius*

With the Sun now also in your solar sixth house you could well begin to develop a sort of perfectionism that is fairly unique to Taurus. Second best probably will not do, and others may have to fall over themselves in order to get things right for you. Maybe you are being just a little too fussy, but woe-betide anyone who says so!

6 MONDAY ☿ *Moon Age Day 6   Moon Sign Sagittarius*

An exciting and adventurous period lies before you this week. There are some really good planetary influences, all of which are urging you onwards towards new incentives and activities. With no time to hang around you can afford to show the world who is boss right now, and few should stand in your way.

7 TUESDAY ☿ *Moon Age Day 7   Moon Sign Capricorn*

You function well when it comes to looking after your own interests, especially in a financial sense. However, it is quite important at the moment that you do not allow your Taurean fondness for detail to get in your way at a time when a broad overview is far more useful. You can obtain any help you need from colleagues.

8 WEDNESDAY ☿ *Moon Age Day 8   Moon Sign Capricorn*

This could be a very confusing and tense time as far as your personal life is concerned, particularly if you fail to look at things in an objective and honest manner. You could easily be worrying about something without any evidence or justification, and that means dissipating otherwise useful energy to no real purpose.

9 THURSDAY ☿ *Moon Age Day 9   Moon Sign Aquarius*

Progress in your career depends on your ability to think down completely new channels. Taurus can certainly be on the ball at the moment but there is a tendency for you to sometimes get stuck in your way of thinking. The more revolutionary you are at present, the greater is the chance that you can get the world at large to take notice.

10 FRIDAY ☿ *Moon Age Day 10   Moon Sign Aquarius*

Make the most of a good period for romance, perhaps by sweeping someone completely off their feet. Social relationships should also be very good and will offer you the chance of new friendships, one or two of which might endure for a very long time. This is not to suggest that you ignore old friends, all of whom remain important.

11 SATURDAY ☿ *Moon Age Day 11   Moon Sign Aquarius*

Trends encourage you to look towards your pals for a good time this weekend. Formal situations are not significant and rather you can make up your mind as you go along when it comes to enjoyment. The more spontaneous you are, the greater is the chance that you make this one of those very special times that cannot be planned.

12 SUNDAY ☿ *Moon Age Day 12   Moon Sign Pisces*

Your critical faculties are excellent and it would take someone very clever indeed to pull the wool over your eyes at the moment. You might decide this is an ideal time for looking at and signing documents of any sort, and for embarking on a new project that is going to demand a great deal of your time and attention in the weeks ahead.

13 MONDAY ☿ *Moon Age Day 13   Moon Sign Pisces*

There are signs that you may be too easily distracted at the start of this working week, and for that you can thank the present position of the Moon. Today and tomorrow represent a period when you can rely more on the good offices of colleagues and friends, whilst you take a short break from being quite as organised as you have been.

14 TUESDAY ☿ *Moon Age Day 14   Moon Sign Aries*

Romantic and social activities can represent a welcome diversion, especially if you are not in the mood to commit yourself exclusively to work. This would be an excellent time to bury the hatchet in any long-standing disagreement or row, and you have what it takes to play the honest broker for others.

15 WEDNESDAY ☿   *Moon Age Day 15   Moon Sign Aries*

Someone you haven't seen for a very long time could now crop up in your life again, possibly by accident. This situation could please you no end and it isn't out of the question that this will be a friend who was once very dear to you. Times change, but the basic nature of people rarely does, as you now have a chance to discover.

16 THURSDAY ☿   *Moon Age Day 16   Moon Sign Taurus*

You work best now when at the centre of lots of activity. The hotter the situation, the better you should enjoy it, and the cut and thrust of life is what can keep you really busy whilst the lunar high is around. Most important of all at present is your ability to get through or around problems that once seemed impossible to solve.

17 FRIDAY   *Moon Age Day 17   Moon Sign Taurus*

This is the time to push boundaries and to try things out before you decide you are not equal to the task. You can achieve victories now that would have seemed absolutely impossible just a short while ago and shouldn't be at all fazed by any sort of opposition. Taurus can afford to be the fearless bull at the moment!

18 SATURDAY   *Moon Age Day 18   Moon Sign Gemini*

Personal relationships and partnerships of all sorts can now offer much more than you bargained for, though generally in a very positive sense. Your powers of attraction are clearly very strong at the moment so don't be afraid to use them to your own advantage. Just don't lead someone up the garden path romantically.

19 SUNDAY   *Moon Age Day 19   Moon Sign Gemini*

The Moon in your solar third house contributes to a period that fires your curiosity in all sorts of ways. You may now decide you want to know what makes everything tick, and might be turning over every stone as you mosey down the path of life. The result might be one or two real surprises and the odd truly delightful situation.

20 MONDAY
Moon Age Day 20   Moon Sign Cancer

You have a very fertile mind at the best of times but now it can be truly active. Intuition is strong and you can afford to back your hunches to a much greater extent than has been the case in the very recent past. Life is now much more about feelings than evidence, though this might be hard for some Taureans to appreciate.

21 TUESDAY
Moon Age Day 21   Moon Sign Cancer

Your administrative talents are especially well starred at present, so if there is something that needs organising, now is the time to get cracking. The same is generally true at home, where you have scope to get things organised ahead of the upcoming winter. Taurus can be a bit of a squirrel and likes to get things comfortable!

22 WEDNESDAY
Moon Age Day 22   Moon Sign Leo

At this time the focus is clearly on your personal life, and even if you remain generally busy in a practical sense, it's worth spending time in the company of your partner, sorting things out and proving the depth of your affection. All this effort will certainly not be wasted and there is great love coming back in your direction.

23 THURSDAY
Moon Age Day 23   Moon Sign Leo

The trends of yesterday continue, helping you to make this a rewarding and happy time when in the company of loved ones. This is not to suggest that your efforts out there in the wider world are diminished, but merely spending time sorting out more personal aspects of your life can work wonders. Younger people could figure significantly now.

24 FRIDAY
Moon Age Day 24   Moon Sign Virgo

You have the ability to think and plan on your feet and Mercury, now in your solar sixth house, certainly helps with this regard. What you come up with now should be useful to all concerned and is certainly a benefit to your friends. Trends support selfless acts, and perhaps almost everything you do is for someone else.

25 SATURDAY
Moon Age Day 25   Moon Sign Virgo

Your strength lies in getting people to notice you this weekend, mainly because of the positive way you express yourself. It is easy to make people feel important and to encourage them to work hard on your behalf. Routines don't appeal, and it's worth ringing the changes whenever possible. A late holiday might be in order.

26 SUNDAY
Moon Age Day 26   Moon Sign Virgo

Your diplomatic and interpersonal skills have rarely been better favoured, and it shouldn't be hard to get onside with just about anyone under present trends. Be prepared to use this to approach someone who has really caused you problems in the past, turning difficulties into opportunities. Another strong social day with the possibility of travel.

27 MONDAY
Moon Age Day 27   Moon Sign Libra

Handling a heavy workload may not bother you at all as this week gets started, though this situation can change significantly as the days go on, so make the most of this positive beginning. By all means clear the decks for actions that come at the far end of the week, but don't plan anything too strenuous for Wednesday or Thursday.

28 TUESDAY
Moon Age Day 28   Moon Sign Libra

Trends assist you to remain productive and capable, though it's possible that one or two people are failing to be quite as helpful or even civil as you might expect. The fault could be on their side, but there is just a chance you are not quite as diplomatic now as was the case only a few days ago. A day to show your compassion and concern.

29 WEDNESDAY
Moon Age Day 0   Moon Sign Scorpio

Basically the lunar low brings a slight downer of a period and a time during which you might decide to take a well-earned break. Even if not everything you do is going wrong, it might be hard to make any significant headway and it might be best not to push yourself at all. Support can be gained from colleagues and friends.

30 THURSDAY   *Moon Age Day 1   Moon Sign Scorpio*

Today could be slightly characterised by confusion – that is, unless you do one job at once and think things through carefully before you commit yourself to anything at all. Fortunately you can make sure there is a great deal of good humour about too, together with the company of people who have the ability to make you laugh out loud.

31 FRIDAY   *Moon Age Day 2   Moon Sign Sagittarius*

The lunar low is now well and truly out of the way and Friday offers more in the way of innovation and inspiration. Your best approach is to split your time between practical necessities and those things you actively want to do. You can show yourself to be quite sporting and more than able to win through in solo or team situations.

November

⑧

2008

1 SATURDAY
Moon Age Day 3   Moon Sign Sagittarius

The changes you make to your finances can give you more ease and comfort in your surroundings, though this is likely to be a gradual process that takes place across the next few weeks. For now there is scope to be happy. Taurus may well be in the mood for a spot of shopping or a trip to visit relatives or friends.

2 SUNDAY
Moon Age Day 4   Moon Sign Sagittarius

A boost to your general level of optimism is possible courtesy of the Moon. If your sense of personal freedom is strong, there won't be much that could hold you back when it comes to pleasing yourself on this November Sunday. A day to leave any worries on the back burner whilst you set out to explore a world that changes all the time.

3 MONDAY
Moon Age Day 5   Moon Sign Capricorn

There is a testing phase on the way for your partnerships, whether these are of a personal or a professional sort. If you are operating more as a solo agent for the moment, that might be part of what is causing the potential problems. This would be out of character, because you are usually so good at sharing.

4 TUESDAY
Moon Age Day 6   Moon Sign Capricorn

The Sun in your solar seventh house can act as a boost to friendships and nullifies to some extent the position of Mars. Group-related matters look much livelier and potentially more successful than they did yesterday, and you might also be much more willing to allow someone else to make a few of the major decisions.

5 WEDNESDAY
Moon Age Day 7   Moon Sign Aquarius

Although there is presently little scope for shortcuts to success, this fact needn't bother you too much. Taurus is used to working hard for what it wants, and whilst others tire easily, you can keep going no matter what. Some Taureans might look a little fragile, but nothing could be further from the truth.

6 THURSDAY
Moon Age Day 8   Moon Sign Aquarius

You could benefit greatly today from getting together with others and discussing almost anything under the sun. Some of the best answers you find at the moment can come as a result of these discussions, and if you are in a very 'think tank' mentality, the more people you draw into your circle, the better the results you can achieve.

7 FRIDAY
Moon Age Day 9   Moon Sign Aquarius

Some Taurus subjects may now decide on significant changes as far as personal relationships are concerned. This is a period stimulated by your ruling planet Venus, which presently occupies your solar eighth house of change. Relationships may take on a new and better feel, or new ones could be started now.

8 SATURDAY
Moon Age Day 10   Moon Sign Pisces

Paradoxically for those of you who do not work at the weekend, today offers some of the very best professional prospects of the week. You can afford to be quite decisive now and not leave anything to chance. Domestic prospects are very slightly less rosy, particularly if those around you are tetchy or inclined to be over-critical about something.

9 SUNDAY
Moon Age Day 11   Moon Sign Pisces

Partnerships are to the fore, especially if you are trying hard to bring someone round to a point of view that seems quite self-evident to you. No matter how hard you try, you may have difficulty persuading someone to follow your lead, and finding a compromise may be your best response.

10 MONDAY
Moon Age Day 12   Moon Sign Aries

With the Moon passing through the quiet solar twelfth house, the impact you make on life is apt to be rather less positive or even noticeable than has been the case. This might not be an entirely bad thing, because there are potentially even busier times ahead, and there could be significant gains from standing still and taking stock.

11 TUESDAY
Moon Age Day 13   Moon Sign Aries

Venus can help you to make personal relationships far more rewarding today and brings a phase during which you can find time to listen to what those closest to you are actually saying. Much of what you hear now seems to make eminent sense, and you can use it to make progress in areas that might have been a problem for while.

12 WEDNESDAY
Moon Age Day 14   Moon Sign Taurus

The arrival of the lunar high encourages your individuality, and you needn't stay in the background. Wherever there is action, that is where you should choose to be, because Taurus is now about as dynamic and driving as it is possible for the zodiac sign to be. Getting your own way could prove to be relatively easy.

13 THURSDAY
Moon Age Day 15   Moon Sign Taurus

You can now show quite unusual ways of responding to what life offers you, with the result that you are living your life in a fairly unique way. The attraction you have for others isn't at all in doubt, and you can turn heads wherever you go. This period isn't all about work because from a social point of view you have what it takes to sizzle!

14 FRIDAY
Moon Age Day 16   Moon Sign Gemini

The big lesson to learn today is that you need to be careful about exerting a possessive influence on those close to you. It may not be the right way forward to try and make them change to suit your wants or needs. In any case you will be more likely to have a positive influence on them if you allow them to decide for themselves.

59

15 SATURDAY   *Moon Age Day 17*   *Moon Sign Gemini*

If you are feeling slightly insecure at the moment, this is part of the reason why you are inclined to be somewhat jealous or possessive. This is the less favourable face of Taurus and something you need to fight against in any situation. With a little effort you can become more giving and understanding, which is the Taurus everyone loves.

16 SUNDAY   *Moon Age Day 18*   *Moon Sign Cancer*

Changeability is an effect of the Moon in your third house, but its position there also encourages you to talk, particularly about emotional and personal matters. Your thinking processes needn't be fixed at the moment and you may well exhibit more of a butterfly mentality than would usually be the case.

17 MONDAY   *Moon Age Day 19*   *Moon Sign Cancer*

A period of some mental pressure is possible at this time, particularly if you have so many choices to make. Try not to dwell too much on specific issues and allow your intuition to be at least part of your guide. This is because your usual common sense might not be enough to get you the answers you need.

18 TUESDAY   *Moon Age Day 20*   *Moon Sign Leo*

Now is a time to be widening your horizons, and it would also be an excellent period for making any sort of journey. Why not contact people you don't see all that often? They can bring with them an entirely different way of looking at issues you thought you had put to bed some time ago.

19 WEDNESDAY   *Moon Age Day 21*   *Moon Sign Leo*

Good communications with relatives and with your partner will probably be needed today if you are to solve a slight problem or series of problems at home. There is a great deal to be said at the moment for sticking with a few routines and also for allowing others to take some of the strain.

20 THURSDAY
Moon Age Day 22   Moon Sign Leo

If you seek out some happy spirits today, you can make the day go with a real swing. Allowing your personality to show its sunnier side could persuade others to have something interesting to say to you. It's as if you realise that good things are going to happen – and hey presto, they do!

21 FRIDAY
Moon Age Day 23   Moon Sign Virgo

Specific issues should not be allowed to become obsessions around now. Remember that your animal sign, the Bull, is a grazer and never stays in the same place for very long. Bear this in mind when it comes to concerns. Have a look at them for a while and then move on. They will probably look less important from a distance.

22 SATURDAY
Moon Age Day 24   Moon Sign Virgo

This might not be the most romantic period of the month, but it does offer certain benefits that do have a bearing on personal attachments. You have what it takes to be a good talker and also a great listener this weekend. If you are attentive, people who tend to have kept things somewhat hidden for a while should now open up.

23 SUNDAY
Moon Age Day 25   Moon Sign Libra

Make the most of a period of distinct emotional release because that is what is on offer at the moment. Issues that have been buried in the past can now be addressed decisively, particularly if you can get others to join in the discussions. Try to get some change into your life later in the day.

24 MONDAY
Moon Age Day 26   Moon Sign Libra

Trends suggest a fairly unsettled period early in the week. If people you meet in a professional or social sense don't seem to be making all that much sense, be prepared to make allowances for them. Nothing seems to be all that reliable and the only time things go the way you would expect is when you attend to them yourself.

25 TUESDAY
Moon Age Day 27   Moon Sign Scorpio

This is a watch and wait period, whilst the Moon passes through your opposite zodiac sign of Scorpio and brings the lunar low for the month. Gambling should probably be avoided for the moment, and you would be much better off sitting on your purse or wallet for now. A time to avoid getting into pointless arguments.

26 WEDNESDAY
Moon Age Day 28   Moon Sign Scorpio

Life can seem fairly demanding, whilst at the same time it may not offer you quite the level of incentives you have come to expect of late. Everything you get seems to come hard, but at least you are applying yourself well and won't be easily beaten. In some situations it might well be the case that you are trying just a little too hard.

27 THURSDAY
Moon Age Day 29   Moon Sign Scorpio

Although the Moon is still in Scorpio at the beginning of today, it soon moves on, leaving you with an afternoon that should be far less complicated and troublesome. Even if everything seems to straighten itself out, all that has really changed is your attitude. Don't worry in advance of something that is actually geared towards your happiness.

28 FRIDAY
Moon Age Day 0   Moon Sign Sagittarius

You should now discover that you have the emotional resources to take on challenges of most sorts. The end of the working week offers a chance to become more committed to specific situations than has been the case for the last few days. Strong social urges are also present and you have scope to make tonight quite special in some way.

29 SATURDAY
Moon Age Day 1   Moon Sign Sagittarius

Venus is now in your solar ninth house and this can assist you to come out of yourself. You are now in a period during which travel of any sort would be both enjoyable and profitable in some way, though you may see family constraints as being a reason not to move around too much. In the end the decision will be yours.

30 SUNDAY   *Moon Age Day 2   Moon Sign Capricorn*

This is another time during which you can capitalise on the ability to do something novel or different. Getting out to places of culture and learning something on the way could prove to be very important to Taurus under present trends. What is more, you can inspire others with your refreshing attitudes and your deep knowledge.

⑧ December
2008

1 MONDAY
Moon Age Day 3   Moon Sign Capricorn

Why not put your detective hat on today? Just about everything interests you, but what stands out is your present rampant curiosity. When it comes to working out why things happen in the way they do you need to leave no stone unturned – and you can also make sure you have a good time on the way.

2 TUESDAY
Moon Age Day 4   Moon Sign Capricorn

Even if you find yourself in a rather taxing role today, trends offer you energy to spare at the moment, so this should not turn out to be too much of a problem. In most situations you appear to know what you are doing, and you also have the ability to bluff your way through when you are not so sure.

3 WEDNESDAY
Moon Age Day 5   Moon Sign Aquarius

The Sun is now in your solar eighth house, as indeed it always is at this time of year for Taurus. This is why late November and the first two thirds of December tend to be an ideal time of year to embark on significant changes. You may not have registered the fact, but it's true and could be especially so this year.

4 THURSDAY
Moon Age Day 6   Moon Sign Aquarius

For a number of planetary reasons your interests are now encouraged to turn towards mental and philosophical considerations. Some Taureans may decide to gain a new spiritual dimension to their lives or else embark on some sort of health kick that brings mental depth as well as stronger muscles. Beware of pushing yourself too hard.

5 FRIDAY
Moon Age Day 7   Moon Sign Pisces

If you are expected to make some fairly heavy compromises at the moment, that may not be all that easy. The fact is that Taurus can be very stubborn and especially so when its most cherished values are at stake. Before digging your heels in today it is worth analysing how important your pride really is.

6 SATURDAY
Moon Age Day 8   Moon Sign Pisces

A new phase is underway and it is one that may challenge you to renew and revitalise certain aspects of your life that have become dull or unworkable. Of necessity this means leaving something behind, and that isn't necessarily easy for Taurus. Excess baggage isn't important though, and it is probably getting in your way.

7 SUNDAY
Moon Age Day 9   Moon Sign Pisces

It may feel today as if everyone is getting on better than you are, but this is nothing but an illusion. Your best approach is to be content with your lot and spend at least some of today looking forward to the Christmas period. For some Taurus subjects this might be the first time that the nearness of the impending festive season has occurred to you.

8 MONDAY
Moon Age Day 10   Moon Sign Aries

Self-criticism at the start of this working week can stem from too great an expectation of yourself and your recent efforts. A more modest approach to situations seems to be called for, together with a greater ability to relax into life. The more content you make yourself, the better most aspects of your life will seem to be.

9 TUESDAY
Moon Age Day 11   Moon Sign Aries

Immediately before the arrival of the lunar high the Moon always passes through your solar twelfth house. This encourages you to be more contemplative and probably more inclined to worry about inconsequential details. Such is the case today. Most problems right now are nothing more than clouds – so why not stand and watch them drift away?

10 WEDNESDAY *Moon Age Day 12   Moon Sign Taurus*

With the lunar high comes fresh opportunities and the greatest dose of optimism you will have experienced so far this month. Be prepared to put your abilities to good use and don't stand around looking at things today. It's time to pitch in, as well as being the right period for telling other people the way you want things to be.

11 THURSDAY *Moon Age Day 13   Moon Sign Taurus*

Today you can discover amazing new talents, and certainly shouldn't be short of refreshing ideas to get life going the way you would wish. You can be very socially inclined so if those festive parties have started early, so much the better. Making a good impression on others might be as easy for you today as falling off a log.

12 FRIDAY *Moon Age Day 14   Moon Sign Gemini*

You may discover today how important it is to plan your next strategy, because certain situations will unravel like a ball of wool if you trust to luck. This need not be a problem because Taurus is about as organised as any zodiac sign can be. Unforced errors are not inevitable, but it is still very necessary to concentrate.

13 SATURDAY *Moon Age Day 15   Moon Sign Gemini*

At this time, getting out and about can prove to be both mentally and physically stimulating. The focus is on meeting new people and seeing things that have passed you by before – even if they are only a stone's throw from your own home! Socially speaking you can be on top form, and romance might also be a significant factor now.

14 SUNDAY *Moon Age Day 16   Moon Sign Cancer*

Trends assist you to get what you want today with the aid of a little persuasion, and you needn't be put off by slightly negative attitudes of people with whom you have to deal. Avoid getting involved in arguments of any sort, but particularly those that you know instinctively are going to lead you nowhere at all.

15 MONDAY
Moon Age Day 17   Moon Sign Cancer

A slight winding down of personal ambitions is the legacy of the Moon now moving into your solar fourth house. For the next couple of days, home-based matters are favoured, and you may not have quite the same urge to travel around that has been obvious for most Taureans of late.

16 TUESDAY
Moon Age Day 18   Moon Sign Leo

The way ahead now looks fairly clear, though you view it from a sort of platform and may not be putting in too much in the way of direct physical effort for the moment. For some days now you should have been ridding yourself of baggage that you don't want to carry forward into the coming year. New incentives are at hand.

17 WEDNESDAY
Moon Age Day 19   Moon Sign Leo

The Moon has moved on and you are not encouraged to stay around home too much now. The time has come for action and for moving about freely in the world at large. Present influences are great for travel and intellectual pursuits of any sort. There will be opportunities today to show how very bright you are.

18 THURSDAY
Moon Age Day 20   Moon Sign Virgo

It would be a great advantage today to continue your general efforts to get on well – but whilst also learning the value of dynamic relaxation. The situation is helped if you tackle one task at a time and don't crowd yourself with tasks that aren't at all necessary. You should also get on better if you learn to delegate.

19 FRIDAY
Moon Age Day 21   Moon Sign Virgo

Today responds best if you make the most of specific beneficial trends that stand around you. Although you are warm, sincere and friendly, it is towards the practical aspects of life that your mind is likely to turn. Many Taureans might relish a shopping spree today – even though the stores will be very crowded.

20 SATURDAY — *Moon Age Day 22   Moon Sign Libra*

You might now have to rethink a pet project very carefully, especially if it is becoming obvious to you that something isn't working in the way you had hoped. There is no point at all in ploughing on regardless, when a slight alteration to the way you behave can make all the difference in a day or two.

21 SUNDAY — *Moon Age Day 23   Moon Sign Libra*

There is no doubt that life could be putting you to the test at present, though not in any way you will find too taxing. If there are puzzles to be solved, that is something you relish. Once again you instinctively seek to know the way everything works and you can ask the right questions that allow you to find out.

22 MONDAY — *Moon Age Day 24   Moon Sign Scorpio*

There is every reason to feel left behind today as you enter the lunar low for December. It might be slightly trying, but at least you will get this less than favourable phase out of the way before Christmas arrives. Don't be afraid to stand and stare for a while, whilst you let other people do some jobs for you. This isn't selfish – it's sensible.

23 TUESDAY — *Moon Age Day 25   Moon Sign Scorpio*

Trends suggest anything but smooth progress, even if the things that go wrong are not really important. Frustrations can be evident and you need to be especially careful if you have to start anything new at this time. Be prepared to seek expert advice from people who really do know what they are talking about, and avoid all cowboys.

24 WEDNESDAY — *Moon Age Day 26   Moon Sign Scorpio*

Even if today starts slowly, you can improve things rapidly as the day moves on. Christmas Eve offers scope to move about again, to be less held back by details and more inclined to get out there and have a good time. Last-minute details can be sorted out and you show a great ability to create fun instantaneously.

25 THURSDAY *Moon Age Day 27 Moon Sign Sagittarius*

Travel is positively highlighted for Christmas Day, so you may decide to spend at least part of the day somewhere other than in your own home. Whether this proves to be the case or not you can remain very cheerful and quite imaginative. Your present attitude is just right for having fun yourself and promoting it for others.

26 FRIDAY *Moon Age Day 28 Moon Sign Sagittarius*

Today is better for intimate relationships and for promoting a greater sense of harmony within your home. Romance can be made to flourish under prevailing trends and you can attract all sorts of compliments from unexpected directions. Stand by to make the Christmas season seem really special for all concerned.

27 SATURDAY *Moon Age Day 0 Moon Sign Capricorn*

If you are involved in discussions today, you could find that the people around you are proving to be more argumentative than you may have expected. You need to keep your patience and to explain yourself as fully as you can. If things still don't go the way you want, you must either compromise or else do your own thing.

28 SUNDAY *Moon Age Day 1 Moon Sign Capricorn*

Along comes a busy period with a definite tendency towards movement and travel. You may decide to visit relatives at a distance or else enliven the holidays by going somewhere special. Whatever you decide to do today it should be something that is as far away from normal routines as you can possibly manage.

29 MONDAY *Moon Age Day 2 Moon Sign Capricorn*

Be open to new input today and allow yourself the right to change your mind if you know instinctively it is necessary to do so. This might involve you in some fairly deep discussions in order to explain yourself, but you can use your silver tongue at the moment and shouldn't have any trouble getting others to agree with you.

30 TUESDAY *Moon Age Day 3   Moon Sign Aquarius*

You certainly needn't be a shrinking violet as the year draws towards its close. Be prepared to get into the social and personal spotlight, as that is where you will undoubtedly feel most comfortable at the moment. Compliments can be attracted from many different directions – though you might be too busy to notice them.

31 WEDNESDAY *Moon Age Day 4   Moon Sign Aquarius*

The Moon is alongside Venus in your solar tenth house today and helps you to make sure that the last day of the year goes extremely well for you. Once again you should be happy to stand out in a crowd and can be the life and soul of any New Year party you decide to attend. What a great way to finish 2008 and to start 2009!

TAURUS:
2009 DIARY PAGES

TAURUS:
2009 IN BRIEF

Expect a fun start to the year and a time during which many of the plans you put on hold late last year can finally come to fruition. January and February give you the chance to work at your full potential and you will be happy to see that others are taking certain situations more seriously. Keep in touch with people you know are in a good position to lend you some timely assistance.

The spring will bring a good deal of excitement and a commitment to change across the board. March and April should find you anxious to keep up the fast pace you are setting yourself and you should be in the market for some positive changes at work. Romance will be playing a bigger part in your life, and there are moments when you really will feel that your popularity is growing by the minute.

The months of May and June are likely to be quieter but will offer you a better opportunity to concentrate on home-based matters. A more solid relationship with family members will be the result, and you will still be in a very romantic frame of mind. Although you may not advance much in a financial sense, you can be fairly certain that when you really do need money, you have the skills to find it.

July and August bring the hottest months of the year for most of us and represent a good opportunity for travel and diversity. You should be happy at this time to move about more and to make the most of exciting opportunities that come your way. Progress is also likely in a professional sense and you could be receiving news that will be both welcome and good from a financial point of view. Avoid getting involved in family feuds at this time.

As the year moves on you begin to become slightly more circumspect and will be quite pleased to listen to the sound advice of colleagues or friends. October and November should find you progressive but steady and willing to plan carefully for your longer-term objectives. Something you have been working towards for a fairly long period could now come to fruition, and you may be in the market for a lengthy journey towards the end of the period.

Most Taurean individuals will be planning well ahead for Christmas this year and much of November and December will be taken up with arrangements of one sort or another. Not that this is your exclusive concern because it is also obvious that you are seeking to get on better and to advance yourself in a career sense. People seek you out for your wisdom and solid common sense – a factor that increases your popularity and affords you more influence generally.

January

2009

1 THURSDAY
Moon Age Day 5   Moon Sign Aquarius

Moderation is the key to success at the start of this particular year. You need time to think things through and to get matters right before you proceed onto the next topic. From a social point of view you do seem to be on good form and have what it takes to impress people. However, you can also afford to enjoy quiet times today.

2 FRIDAY
Moon Age Day 6   Moon Sign Pisces

Whatever happens today could help to widen your social horizons, particularly if you remain in a more approachable frame of mind. The Sun is presently in your solar ninth house, which is going to be useful when it comes to interesting news. Snippets of information can be sought from many different places.

3 SATURDAY
Moon Age Day 7   Moon Sign Pisces

With Venus now in your solar tenth house you do have the best possible opportunity to mix business with pleasure. You have scope to glean interesting ideas and useful information from almost anyone you meet. Of course there are always going to be exceptions but it would be best to completely avoid those who prove difficult.

4 SUNDAY
Moon Age Day 8   Moon Sign Aries

A professional environment would offer you plenty of freedom today, though of course there is a good chance that you will not be working on a Sunday. All aspects of leisure and pleasure are favoured as well, and you could be happiest of all curled up in your favourite chair, away from the cold winter weather.

5 MONDAY
Moon Age Day 9   Moon Sign Aries

With the Moon now in your solar twelfth house you may decide to withdraw from the rough and tumble of life, but don't worry because this is a very short interlude indeed. By tomorrow, you can bring everything together, and today would be best seen as a time to get yourself ready for what is likely to be a big onslaught.

6 TUESDAY
Moon Age Day 10   Moon Sign Taurus

Today the Moon enters your own zodiac sign, bringing that period known as the lunar high. Make the most of the energy available, and the chance to prove yourself in any one of a hundred different ways. Spontaneity is the key to bringing joy into the lives of others, as well as into your own.

7 WEDNESDAY
Moon Age Day 11   Moon Sign Taurus

Things should continue to go well for you and you have what it takes to keep Lady Luck on your side. In your dealings with others you show yourself to be considerate and caring – something that doesn't go unnoticed. Routines won't interest you today because the focus is on forging new pathways.

8 THURSDAY
Moon Age Day 12   Moon Sign Gemini

Culture and the possibility of travel are well accented at the moment. You should still be feeling pretty much on top form and needn't stand in the shadows. Although Taurus can sometimes be hesitant or shy, this isn't the impression you should be giving to the world at large throughout the remainder of this particular week.

9 FRIDAY
Moon Age Day 13   Moon Sign Gemini

Make the most of harmonious trends to improve your social life. It looks as though you can get people on your side and persuade them to help you get on in life. You tend to respond in kind and you will be doing as many favours as you can. If some jobs seem endless, simply plough on in your own sweet way.

10 SATURDAY   *Moon Age Day 14   Moon Sign Cancer*

A time to take full advantage of your abilities when it comes to communicating. You have what it takes to make this a very social sort of weekend and to make a good impression on people who can be useful to you in one way or another. In specific tasks it might be necessary to get back to basics and to start again if you have to.

11 SUNDAY   *Moon Age Day 15   Moon Sign Cancer*

Exciting things are on offer, but you will have to look carefully if you want to get the very best out of what today has available. Relationships are especially well starred right now and Taurus individuals who have been looking for new love should concentrate their efforts around this time. New friendships are also possible.

12 MONDAY   *Moon Age Day 16   Moon Sign Leo*

Your mental processes are very sharp at the beginning of this week and you shouldn't have to try very hard in order to get ahead. An ideal time to contact those you don't see very often, and to make the most of what they have to offer. Long-term plans can be dealt with easily at this time.

13 TUESDAY   ☿   *Moon Age Day 17   Moon Sign Leo*

New information is at hand and you should get right to the front of the queue when it comes to making the most of whatever is going. You have scope to be ingenious and imaginative, two qualities that can stand you in good stead under present planetary trends. Acting on impulse socially helps you to create some good times.

14 WEDNESDAY ☿   *Moon Age Day 18   Moon Sign Virgo*

You needn't hide your light under a bushel at this time. If there is something you know, you should be willing to speak out, no matter what company you happen to be in. Taurus can be both active and enterprising now, and you have what it takes to get ahead professionally and in a social sense. Money matters are variable, but can be improved.

15 THURSDAY ☿ *Moon Age Day 19 Moon Sign Virgo*

Venus remains in your solar eleventh house, which is especially good as far as your social life is concerned. Once again it becomes more than possible to mix business with pleasure and to show your best face to practically everyone you meet. You have what it takes to make this a very happy day – made better by your constant smile.

16 FRIDAY ☿ *Moon Age Day 20 Moon Sign Libra*

You are a person who relishes being on the move and exploring new territory and under present trends that is exactly what you have a chance to do. You might not enjoy the winter weather because you were born under a spring zodiac sign, but you can get wrapped up, and should generate plenty of personal warmth from within!

17 SATURDAY ☿ *Moon Age Day 21 Moon Sign Libra*

It's worth disciplining yourself right now in order to defer gratification in certain areas until later. Do your best to finish difficult or tedious tasks first and then you will leave time for later, when you can do exactly what takes your fancy. An early start to the day would be good – that way you will feel pleased with all you manage to achieve.

18 SUNDAY ☿ *Moon Age Day 22 Moon Sign Libra*

Things could be slowing down somewhat as today advances, but the reason for this state of affairs won't become totally apparent until tomorrow. Tell yourself that this is a Sunday and that you don't have to work too hard in any case. Social trends are still good and there should be plenty of opportunity for mixing and mingling.

19 MONDAY ☿ *Moon Age Day 23 Moon Sign Scorpio*

This may not be the best possible start to a new week because the Moon has now moved into your opposite zodiac sign of Scorpio. This period, which comes around each month, is known as the lunar low. Even if you are listless and lacking in your usual common sense, you still have what it takes to get others working for you.

20 TUESDAY ☿ *Moon Age Day 24 Moon Sign Scorpio*

Patience is the key to dealing with the demands that are made of you at this time, particularly if you are dealing with individuals who seem to have no real sense of their own. The real frustration might come from having to start the same job time and again – though Taurean patience is legendary, and very useful now.

21 WEDNESDAY ☿ *Moon Age Day 25 Moon Sign Sagittarius*

All of a sudden things change. The lunar low has moved away and now you are under the strong influence of a tenth-house Sun. Be prepared to develop a 'can do' attitude to life and to take on new responsibilities. You can use the positive responses of others to make a delight out of usually tedious jobs.

22 THURSDAY ☿ *Moon Age Day 26 Moon Sign Sagittarius*

Social developments are favoured and your ruling planet, Venus, proves to be especially helpful to you around this time. When it comes to romance you should be able to find the right words to sweep someone off their feet and you shouldn't stick fast when it comes to making important gestures. There is little wonder you can make everyone love you!

23 FRIDAY ☿ *Moon Age Day 27 Moon Sign Sagittarius*

It is intellectual exchanges that can make this particular day special, and it looks as though you could mix comfortably with just about anyone. New health regimes are possible and you may decide to give up something you know hasn't been doing you much good. On the professional front you can still manage to turn heads.

24 SATURDAY ☿ *Moon Age Day 28 Moon Sign Capricorn*

Why not turn towards creative and imaginative ideas for the weekend? If the day is your own and you are not working, you can afford to 'waste' a little time today. In the end nothing is wasted because you can turn leisure and pleasure to your distinct advantage. It's worth keeping abreast of current affairs today and reading the local paper.

25 SUNDAY ☿ *Moon Age Day 29   Moon Sign Capricorn*

Now there is much to be said for new mental interests and from pushing your mind further than might normally be the case. You might excel in any sort of quiz, and even if you don't walk away with first prize, you can impress people. An ideal day to spend some time with your lover and find those special words that mean so much.

26 MONDAY ☿ *Moon Age Day 0   Moon Sign Aquarius*

You may find this is one of the better days of the month for busy preparations. Keep an eye on the clock, particularly if there is much to be done and only you to do it. Of course you could turn some jobs over to others, but you need to consider whether they would perform to your exacting standards.

27 TUESDAY ☿ *Moon Age Day 1   Moon Sign Aquarius*

Your verbal skills are well starred, which together with a few positive planetary trends might make this the best time of all for asking for a rise in salary. What you have to tell yourself is that those in authority can only say no and they might say yes. It's time for Taurus to show its natural courage.

28 WEDNESDAY ☿ *Moon Age Day 2   Moon Sign Aquarius*

You are in the middle of an excellent time for promoting yourself – something that goes far beyond professional matters. You can excel in romance and friendship and could give anyone a run for their money when in open competition. Some of the gains you are able to make today may not even be in your mind when you get out of bed.

29 THURSDAY ☿ *Moon Age Day 3   Moon Sign Pisces*

The time is still right to pursue ideas that can broaden your horizons in a general sense. Be careful though, because assuming you are right about everything is not the best way forward, and you could make an enemy or two if you show yourself as being too pushy. Your usual modesty is what sets you apart and is what people love.

30 FRIDAY ☿ *Moon Age Day 4   Moon Sign Pisces*

You can now reap all the benefits of teamwork – whether in a professional or a social sense. Family members can be somewhat trying at present, particularly if what they want for their own lives is not what you would wish on their behalf. A compromise or two could be called for, so why not start the ball rolling?

31 SATURDAY ☿ *Moon Age Day 5   Moon Sign Aries*

An ideal time to enjoy sharing interesting ideas and swapping stories with just about anyone who is willing to listen. You have scope to turn casual acquaintances into close friends and perhaps to move in slightly different circles. New interests are well accented around this time.

⑧ February
2009

1 SUNDAY
Moon Age Day 6   Moon Sign Aries

The first day of a new month brings tests as far as your inner strength is concerned and this is when you can really begin to shine. As a Taurean you can be courageous and quite determined. Even your natural stubbornness is not always a bad thing, as you may now discover. Keep up your efforts to sort out the lives of younger relatives.

2 MONDAY
Moon Age Day 7   Moon Sign Taurus

Right now you have an opportunity to express your individuality and to use your competitive instincts to the full. Woe-betide anyone who tries to get the better of you under present planetary trends. At a more personal level you can show a kind and caring side to your nature, but this may not be obvious out there in the wider world.

3 TUESDAY
Moon Age Day 8   Moon Sign Taurus

The lunar high is now in full force, and you have what it takes to knock down any number of obstacles that have been blocking your path in the recent past. You can persuade friends and colleagues to give support, particularly if you have the bit between your teeth. You know what you want – and why.

4 WEDNESDAY
Moon Age Day 9   Moon Sign Taurus

Being right is of special importance to you today and you continue to push forward very progressively. You can keep Lady Luck on your side and use your special gift for getting it right first time. Taurus doesn't usually act on impulse but in many respects you are a special sort of Taurean whilst the lunar high is present.

5 THURSDAY · *Moon Age Day 10* · *Moon Sign Gemini*

Mars is now in your solar tenth house and this allows you to use your vigorous energy to positively attack work that needs skill and precision. All the same it would be sensible to curb a tendency for getting everything done at the same time. Slow and steady is the way of the Bull, though it might not seem that way today.

6 FRIDAY · *Moon Age Day 11* · *Moon Sign Gemini*

You could find that at least some of what happens today is not in your best interest. Your associations with others can be somewhat strained and you might show less patience than would normally be the case. Avoid situations that sound too good to be true, because at the end of the day this is what they will turn out to be.

7 SATURDAY · *Moon Age Day 12* · *Moon Sign Cancer*

Prospects look generally good for the weekend, offering you a chance to show a friendlier and calmer face to the world at large. Mars is still helping you along but you can be more in control of the situation now and happy to allow others to take the lead in at least some matters. In sporting activities there is now everything to play for.

8 SUNDAY · *Moon Age Day 13* · *Moon Sign Cancer*

It could remain difficult for you to enjoy situations that are led by individuals you see as being incompetent. This is the influence of that tenth-house Mars. In the main you want to be the innovator and to have the last say about almost anything. Such a state of affairs is unusual for Taurus and friends might wonder what is wrong with you.

9 MONDAY · *Moon Age Day 14* · *Moon Sign Leo*

With Venus now occupying your twelfth house there is a slight risk that your love life will be in the doldrums – or at the very least less than inspiring. You can do something about this by making what are usually instinctive gestures to your partner more thought-out. Be prepared to give attention to friends.

10 TUESDAY
Moon Age Day 15   Moon Sign Leo

It looks as though all that Taurean charm is now beginning to return – at least in the short term. The position of the Moon today can be helpful in terms of your charisma, and you have scope to gain a high degree of popularity. How much good this will do you on a normal working day remains to be seen, but general trends are also good.

11 WEDNESDAY
Moon Age Day 16   Moon Sign Virgo

At work you may be demanding specific and very important changes. Whether you can get everyone to fall in line with your plans remains to be seen, but you can be quite forceful at the moment and may not take no for an answer regarding issues you see as being important. For Taurus at the moment that could be just about all of them!

12 THURSDAY
Moon Age Day 17   Moon Sign Virgo

The focus is on quickening your pace and making the most of a frenetic interlude. If there is little time to simply sit and take stock, you need to force short periods of reflection if you are not to exhaust yourself. You may not take too kindly to receiving instruction from others – especially those you don't really trust.

13 FRIDAY
Moon Age Day 18   Moon Sign Libra

This is a time to expand your horizons by increasing your general understanding. Gains can be made in fairly unexpected directions, and you may not be ready for all the chances on offer. Reacting to situations quickly is not always your thing but you can be quite responsive under present trends.

14 SATURDAY
Moon Age Day 19   Moon Sign Libra

Weekend-working Taureans can capitalise on endless possibilities for advancement, and all people born under the Bull should be on the lookout for advantages at this time. The start of the weekend offers good social trends and scope to expand your horizons. As a result you may be moving about a good deal.

15 SUNDAY　　*Moon Age Day 20　Moon Sign Scorpio*

If it suddenly seems as though you are carrying a heavy load in terms of responsibilities, you need to be aware that the lunar low is around. How you feel about life and the way things really are can be too entirely different things. This is nothing but a short interlude and one through which you can get useful and needed rest.

16 MONDAY　　*Moon Age Day 21　Moon Sign Scorpio*

On the way up the ladder of success you could find other people or awkward situations blocking your way. Instead of reacting, why not relax? Tomorrow will bring gradually better trends and you will then be able to get back on course. For the moment you could gain from spending valuable moments in a lover's embrace.

17 TUESDAY　　*Moon Age Day 22　Moon Sign Scorpio*

Even if the start of today doesn't prove exciting or stimulating, you can gradually change things as the hours pass. By the afternoon you should be back on course, and that positive position of Mars in your solar chart takes over again. A little impatience might not be a bad thing today, particularly if it helps you get things done.

18 WEDNESDAY　*Moon Age Day 23　Moon Sign Sagittarius*

Stimulation is on offer through your career, and your social life may also be on the up. Tasks that you take on can be sorted in half the normal time and you should feel for the first time in a number of days that you are fully in command of yourself. Be prepared to take the demands of others in your stride.

19 THURSDAY　　*Moon Age Day 24　Moon Sign Sagittarius*

This could be a good day to start an early spring-clean. Although there is a very practical side to this, you can also focus on your own mind. It's time to dump things that are no longer any use to you and to replace them with interesting and stimulating possibilities. Trends encourage thoughts of travel.

20 FRIDAY
Moon Age Day 25   Moon Sign Capricorn

Fulfilment is now found in a sense of personal freedom and in the chance to do what takes your fancy. The time is right to get the routines out of the way early in the day and then set out on some sort of journey – even if it is only a journey of the mind. The weekend lies ahead, and plans made now can mature nicely across the next two days.

21 SATURDAY
Moon Age Day 26   Moon Sign Capricorn

Social relationships can be the source of some light relief, particularly if you avoid the pressures of the world for a day or two. Socially speaking you will be on fine form and you will be well suited to mixing with a variety of different sorts of people. Your charitable instincts are also well highlighted under present trends.

22 SUNDAY
Moon Age Day 27   Moon Sign Capricorn

It isn't putting in endless effort that matters at the moment but rather being clever that counts. Taurus can be very ingenious, and never more so than right now. Be prepared to focus on planning ahead, especially regarding journeys for the future, and also take time out to get in touch with people who live far away or who you don't see very often.

23 MONDAY
Moon Age Day 28   Moon Sign Aquarius

Venus now occupies your solar twelfth house and so in an emotional sense things could be rather low key for a while. If there are issues about that you need to put away once and for all, a discussion might be required. After that, you can afford to leave the past where it belongs.

24 TUESDAY
Moon Age Day 29   Moon Sign Aquarius

An expansion of responsibilities could leave you feeling that you are solely in charge and that colleagues don't want to know. However, there are gains to be made if it enables you to get noticed by people who count. Don't take on more than you can reasonably handle, but do jobs you have to undertake with your usual thoroughness.

25 WEDNESDAY   *Moon Age Day 0   Moon Sign Pisces*

Beneficial trends regarding major ambitions are only going to get stronger at the moment. That's probably a good thing because there is something of an emotional vacuum around at the moment, and your personal life may not be everything you would wish. Most of your life today might revolve around practicalities.

26 THURSDAY   *Moon Age Day 1   Moon Sign Pisces*

You should be making the most of friendship at this stage of the week, and even if you are not quite as responsive as would normally be the case, can make sure you are well liked and respected. It is often the case that others have a greater love of you than you do of yourself. Just listening to what people say could make you feel instantly happier!

27 FRIDAY   *Moon Age Day 2   Moon Sign Aries*

It might be wise to assume a fairly low profile as far as your love life is concerned. The Moon is in your solar twelfth house ahead of the lunar high that arrives early next week. From a physical point of view you have what it takes to be on top form, but you may decide to put your emotional responses on hold for now.

28 SATURDAY   *Moon Age Day 3   Moon Sign Aries*

Today ambitions and goals are not really central to your purpose. Strong social instincts surround you on all sides and what could really work right now is to be in the company of your friends. A shopping spree might be good, but you may not find the sort of bargains that are likely to be on offer from Monday onwards.

♉ March
2009

1 SUNDAY
Moon Age Day 4   Moon Sign Aries

Be prepared to welcome someone from the past back into your life and to make the most of new possibilities for having fun. As the day progresses you get closer to the lunar high, which is likely to be very potent this time around. You could sense a definite easing of emotional tension and a stronger desire to speak your mind.

2 MONDAY
Moon Age Day 5   Moon Sign Taurus

You gain today from being courageous and active, both natural qualities for you but heightened by the presence of the lunar high. Good luck is there for the taking, and you can afford to take a few of the sort of chances you might normally leave alone. What also helps is getting your emotional life back on course.

3 TUESDAY
Moon Age Day 6   Moon Sign Taurus

This wonderful trend gives you more sway regarding loved ones and definite encouragement to break through barriers and into new territories. At work you might be being watched closely, and if you are reacting very positively to responsibility people should like what they see. Your social impulses are extremely strong at this time.

4 WEDNESDAY
Moon Age Day 7   Moon Sign Gemini

You should be able to persuade others to lighten your load now by lending a timely helping hand. Whether or not you decide to do this remains to be seen because you are fairly self-possessed at the moment. All the same you should recognise the care that people generally are showing and can afford to respond in kind.

5 THURSDAY
Moon Age Day 8   Moon Sign Gemini

Venus remains in your solar twelfth house, and in the absence of some of the stronger trends that have predominated across the last few days you may be inclined to daydream a good deal. There's nothing wrong with that, just as long as you stick to genuine possibilities. That way, dreams can be turned to practical use.

6 FRIDAY
Moon Age Day 9   Moon Sign Cancer

Your community spirit is generally strong, and current trends assist you to lend a hand in a charitable sense or in some way that benefits your community. People could well approach you for advice, and even if you feel you are less than qualified to oblige you should at least listen. That's the most important part.

7 SATURDAY
Moon Age Day 10   Moon Sign Cancer

The present position of little Mercury favours communication and also helps you to be in the know when it really matters. Very little is likely to pass you by, either today or tomorrow, and if there is something that really takes your fancy at the moment it is probably to have a good chat with someone interesting.

8 SUNDAY
Moon Age Day 11   Moon Sign Leo

The time has come to take on board a higher social profile. If people want to put you in charge of something it is because they feel you are right for the job. Even if you doubt yourself, others may have supreme confidence in you. Affairs of the heart should be looking up and your emotional responses are gradually becoming steadier.

9 MONDAY
Moon Age Day 12   Moon Sign Leo

You have scope to exude a personal magnetism today that others could find hard to ignore. This is the best time of all for getting what you want and for bringing people round to your point of view. All group activities benefit from this trend and the position of Mercury in your chart right now will enhance your silver-tongued eloquence.

10 TUESDAY
Moon Age Day 13   Moon Sign Virgo

Trends assist you to remain very sociable and warm when dealing with people generally. This is Taurus at its best, and your charity-minded attitude should be much noticed. It would be best today to get tedious or boring jobs out of the way before you commit yourself to tasks you relish that will take up much of your thinking power.

11 WEDNESDAY
Moon Age Day 14   Moon Sign Virgo

Your strength lies in remaining socially adept and you have a host of planetary positions that add to your general friendly attitude. Be prepared to offer help to family members, and to people who are less well off than you find yourself to be.

12 THURSDAY
Moon Age Day 15   Moon Sign Libra

If someone is trying to put the dampener on things, the best thing you can do is to ignore them and to carry on in your own sweet way. You may decide you are better off on your own today, at least when it comes to work. It's worth it if you can avoid the problems and negative attitudes of others.

13 FRIDAY
Moon Age Day 16   Moon Sign Libra

The major asset you have at present is dynamism, together with an ability to keep going when others fall by the wayside. There is no astrological sign as determined as Taurus can be, and although it sometimes takes a while for you to get going, once you do there isn't another person or a force on earth that can stop your progress.

14 SATURDAY
Moon Age Day 17   Moon Sign Libra

Consideration for the feelings of others might dissuade you from taking significant steps towards a chosen objective. You can get round this potential problem by talking to individuals concerned and explaining what you intend to do. It is unlikely that you would be refused any reasonable request under present trends.

15 SUNDAY   *Moon Age Day 18   Moon Sign Scorpio*

Beware of taking too much on today because the lunar low is around, doing little for your strength and endurance. You can't solve all problems yourself and quite frankly you would be better off calling in a few favours and letting friends take some of the daily strain. Meanwhile, why not put your feet up for once?

16 MONDAY   *Moon Age Day 19   Moon Sign Scorpio*

There can be a slight downside to romance at the start of this particular week, but any apparent difficulties exist more in your mind than in reality. Remember to keep people informed of your present mindset because if you fail to do so you could run into difficulties that are exacerbated by the lunar low.

17 TUESDAY   *Moon Age Day 20   Moon Sign Sagittarius*

A new period of rewarding times on the social scene is brought about by little Mercury, which together with the present position of the Sun also assists you to get your own way. There are many different ways you can explain yourself to others, and finding the right approach for the right individual is what today is about.

18 WEDNESDAY   *Moon Age Day 21   Moon Sign Sagittarius*

You can capitalise on an improved social and romantic lifestyle at this time. Gaining new friendships and getting the approval of colleagues or bosses should also be possible. What you don't need at the moment is others telling you how every detail of your life should be arranged. If this happens, it's worth putting the person responsible straight.

19 THURSDAY   *Moon Age Day 22   Moon Sign Capricorn*

Even casual encounters with others today can help you to glean new and improved ideas regarding your own progress for the future. Be prepared to listen carefully to what others have to say, and don't ignore even casual remarks until you have thought about them. Your mind remains extremely active and good ideas are possible at any time.

20 FRIDAY
Moon Age Day 23   Moon Sign Capricorn

Future prospects continue to look good, and there is a particular focus on social developments. Potential disputes with loved ones may demand patience but if you refuse to get annoyed you will win out in the end. Look out for important messages from those who are close.

21 SATURDAY
Moon Age Day 24   Moon Sign Capricorn

With thoughts of your career put on hold for a couple of days, those Taurus individuals who can call the weekend their own can get fully involved in social activities. At the same time you also have a very good eye for a bargain at present, and so maybe a shopping spree would be an idea for today or tomorrow.

22 SUNDAY
Moon Age Day 25   Moon Sign Aquarius

The time is right to seek out interesting and thought-provoking people. It's a fact that you can be very committed to progress at the moment and should use any means at your disposal to get ahead. This shows you being more up-front than might sometimes be the case, and there is no place for Taurean shyness!

23 MONDAY
Moon Age Day 26   Moon Sign Aquarius

This is a time when your influence over everyday matters may be constrained. The Sun is now in your solar twelfth house, where it will remain for the next few weeks. There will be times when it seems as though you are failing to make the progress you wish, but behind the scenes things could be happening to a greater extent than you think.

24 TUESDAY
Moon Age Day 27   Moon Sign Pisces

Venus joins the Sun in your twelfth house, bringing a different sort of constraint for a while. It might be slightly less easy to say what you really think or to find the right words to modify the opinions of family members. In some ways you can feel happier in your own little world, but this may not really be the best place to be this week.

25 WEDNESDAY   *Moon Age Day 28   Moon Sign Pisces*

Social discussions and important decisions are part of what today has to offer. Even if you don't feel quite as confident to make up your mind as was the case earlier in the month, with good support and sound common sense you can get on well enough. It's worth keeping abreast of current affairs and taking an interest in your locality.

26 THURSDAY   *Moon Age Day 0   Moon Sign Pisces*

In terms of general progress it might sometimes seem as if things are not going entirely the way you would wish. A good way forward would be to ride certain changes and to go with the flow as much as possible. Don't expect miracles at this time, but on the other hand be prepared to make the most of any that do come along!

27 FRIDAY   *Moon Age Day 1   Moon Sign Aries*

Your capacity for sound judgement can be somewhat diminished, which is why it might not be sensible to spend large amounts of money today unless you know extremely well what you are doing – and why. Your best approach is to pause for thought and seek the advice of people who may know better than you do.

28 SATURDAY   *Moon Age Day 2   Moon Sign Aries*

Ahead of the lunar high, which comes along tomorrow, you need to plan carefully. You can make this a very social sort of weekend, though on the other hand you might decide to spend more time at home, sorting out issues that have been on your mind for quite some time. A more active Taurean is coming along soon.

29 SUNDAY   *Moon Age Day 3   Moon Sign Taurus*

You have scope to think more ambitiously than has been the case during the last week or so and to put right a few little mistakes. These may not be yours, and it is also possible that family issues will be at the forefront of your mind. Do something that makes this Sunday truly your own. A little comfort would be good.

30 MONDAY
Moon Age Day 4   Moon Sign Taurus

You should now be in a position to take a risk or two, and although the lunar high cannot overpower that twelfth-house Sun, you can do yourself a lot of good. One thing you won't want at the moment is to be told by others how you should behave. Anyone who really has a go at you could be in for a rude awakening!

31 TUESDAY
Moon Age Day 5   Moon Sign Gemini

Now is the time to make sure your plans and ideas take on a practical form and to use any difficulties you have been encountering to sharpen your intellect and your determination. Get on with projects you started earlier in the month and be willing to put in that extra bit of effort that you know can make all the difference.

April

2009

1 WEDNESDAY
Moon Age Day 6   Moon Sign Gemini

You are hardly one for compromise at the beginning of a new month, and needn't take no for an answer if you know you can succeed at something important. You fare best in solo pursuits or when you are in command. In the main you will expect others to follow your lead, and you may not be especially patient if they fail to do so.

2 THURSDAY
Moon Age Day 7   Moon Sign Cancer

Much is now centred on mental activities, and your mind can be as sharp as a razor. You can use it to work out details that others find difficult to even comprehend, and to look at life in a very logical and thorough manner. Information exchange is very important, so be prepared to communicate.

3 FRIDAY
Moon Age Day 8   Moon Sign Cancer

If you feel that something is missing today it will be up to you to fill in the gaps. You remain very astute and filled with a sense of enterprise. Not everyone has it within themselves to understand the way your mind is working, and there may not be too much time for explanations. Later in the day the focus is on love.

4 SATURDAY
Moon Age Day 9   Moon Sign Leo

The Sun remains in your solar twelfth house for a week or two yet, and there are occasions when you may feel as if you are treading water. Even if major aims and objectives have to wait, they could turn out better because of the fine-tuning you are able to bring to them. A whole host of discoveries and delights is there for the taking.

5 SUNDAY
Moon Age Day 10   Moon Sign Leo

This may be a slack period as far as some plans are concerned but it is clear that your powers of communication have rarely been better. People love to have you around at the best of times, but for the moment you seem to be the pick of the social bunch. Conforming to some social expectations may not be as easy as you thought.

6 MONDAY
Moon Age Day 11   Moon Sign Virgo

Right now it seems you are very eager to please, and especially those who are dear to your heart. Taurus is one of the kinder signs of the zodiac and current trends support this. You have scope to shift heaven and earth to do someone a favour, and the fact is not lost on them. Stand by to make the most of some big favours.

7 TUESDAY
Moon Age Day 12   Moon Sign Virgo

An ideal day to seek support for your particular tastes and opinions from some fairly unexpected directions. Loved ones could prove to be rather troublesome later in the day, and you may need to be just a little more severe than you are really feeling. Patience is the keyword at work, and you should avoid over-reactions.

8 WEDNESDAY
Moon Age Day 13   Moon Sign Virgo

Not all your attitudes at the moment may be orthodox, and that could get you into a little trouble with certain individuals. Nevertheless, if you are certain of your ground you can afford to stick to what you believe. Even if you make one or two adversaries on the way, you can bring such people round with your sincerity.

9 THURSDAY
Moon Age Day 14   Moon Sign Libra

In a work sense there is a more progressive and potentially rewarding period at hand. You can gain support for your more ambitious plans from fairly unexpected directions and it might become obvious that certain people have been watching you very closely. In some jobs you will work much better when on your own.

10 FRIDAY *Moon Age Day 15   Moon Sign Libra*

Confidence may not be quite as high today, probably because the lunar low is approaching. All the same you should remain happy enough when dealing with matters you understand. It is the unexpected or the frankly surprising that could shake your sensibilities right now – together with astonishing behaviour from others.

11 SATURDAY *Moon Age Day 16   Moon Sign Scorpio*

A potential lull has now begun, but if things are not exactly inspiring generally during the first half of this month you might not notice it very much. It could offer the chance to settle for a quiet sort of weekend and one during which you can simply please yourself. Be prepared to fall in line with friends regarding social matters.

12 SUNDAY *Moon Age Day 17   Moon Sign Scorpio*

If things go wrong at the moment you would be wise to stop thinking so much and to take time out to recharge your batteries. Plans made for almost any time after the 20th or 21st of this month stand a good chance of working out as you would wish, though in the meantime there could be obstacles about, and more care is necessary.

13 MONDAY *Moon Age Day 18   Moon Sign Sagittarius*

If there is one thing that sets you apart at this time it is your ability to cut through red tape and to see right to the heart of any matter. You prefer things to be simple and uncluttered, and should be doing all you can to demystify certain aspects of your life. That may not go down well with those who have an interest in complicating things.

14 TUESDAY *Moon Age Day 19   Moon Sign Sagittarius*

Personal fulfilment on your part now begins to lie in widened horizons and places you haven't been before. This isn't simply an invitation to travel in a physical sense but to allow your mind more freedom. Trends support anything that is stimulating and cultural at the moment, as well as opportunities to be with intelligent people.

95

15 WEDNESDAY   *Moon Age Day 20   Moon Sign Sagittarius*

The focus is on giving and self-sacrifice today – though there isn't anything especially unusual about this for a Taurean subject. If you are moved by the problems of others you can also be thinking up practical steps that can be taken to help them out. This is true both in your vicinity and in the wider world.

16 THURSDAY   *Moon Age Day 21   Moon Sign Capricorn*

There is much to be said for spending time in the company of people who have very similar backgrounds and motivations to your own. Be prepared to glean inspiration from colleagues, and as the Sun begins to near a more positive place in your solar chart, to allow your level of confidence to rise.

17 FRIDAY   *Moon Age Day 22   Moon Sign Capricorn*

You could be somewhat at odds with a particular type of person today. This is because you support the underdog and hate unfairness or bullying. If speaking out about injustice is something you can't avoid doing, that could get you into a little bother. Not that the fear of contradiction need worry you at all.

18 SATURDAY   *Moon Age Day 23   Moon Sign Aquarius*

Life can be given a faster tempo now that Mercury has moved into your solar first house. Your need to communicate is highlighted, especially when you are in group situations. The weekend can be great fun, but at the same time as you enjoy yourself you can be learning and pushing forward progressively.

19 SUNDAY   *Moon Age Day 24   Moon Sign Aquarius*

Personal objectives and ambitions could now receive small setbacks – but not for very long. In a day or two the Sun moves out of your twelfth solar house and into your first. When it does you can capitalise on opportunities for action and on enhanced enthusiasm. For the moment, why not just bide your time?

20 MONDAY   *Moon Age Day 25   Moon Sign Aquarius*

This is a potentially good time to go out and make new friends. There are bonuses on offer that will be fed by social activity and you should have little or no difficulty mixing business with pleasure. It's worth keeping abreast of what family members are up to. This is especially true in the case of younger relatives or those lacking experience.

21 TUESDAY   *Moon Age Day 26   Moon Sign Pisces*

Don't be afraid to show self-restraint in your social connections, though not because things are likely to be going wrong. On the contrary, the only reason you need to slow things down today is so that you don't totally exhaust yourself. Keeping up with the Joneses might seem very important now – but of course it isn't.

22 WEDNESDAY   *Moon Age Day 27   Moon Sign Pisces*

Mercury becomes stronger in your solar first house, where it waits with baited breath for the Sun to arrive. The potentials of life are extremely good, and you have what it takes to get others to lend you a hand. Even if not everyone is on your side, the people who matter are likely to want the best for you.

23 THURSDAY   *Moon Age Day 28   Moon Sign Aries*

What an excellent time this would be for starting new projects. Positive influences abound and the Sun has at last entered your solar first house. However, it's not worth pushing yourself too hard, and you may decide to allow others to make at least some of the running.

24 FRIDAY   *Moon Age Day 29   Moon Sign Aries*

Trends strengthen your desire to get ahead, though you might still feel that there is something holding you back. Be careful in your dealings with others because there could be someone who is doing their best to lead you up the garden path. Rules and regulations may well get on your nerves at some stage today.

25 SATURDAY   *Moon Age Day 0   Moon Sign Taurus*

At last everything is lined up at the same time to offer you the very best potential. The lunar high encourages you to announce your abilities and your capabilities to the whole world, and to put yourself right at the front of the queue when it comes to making yourself known. There is plenty of good luck on offer at present.

26 SUNDAY   *Moon Age Day 1   Moon Sign Taurus*

Confidence in your abilities should improve markedly, and you have scope to make this a weekend to remember. The bigger your ideas are at the moment, the better they are likely to work out for you. Keep looking and listening today because even the most mundane of conversations can lead you on to greater potential.

27 MONDAY   *Moon Age Day 2   Moon Sign Gemini*

Influences regarding personal attachments could be somewhat disappointing at the beginning of this particular week. It is possible that certain individuals will let you down and that could lead to more work being necessary on your part. At the same time you can be fairly shrewd, so loss-limitation is part of the Taurean brief right now.

28 TUESDAY   *Moon Age Day 3   Moon Sign Gemini*

At last you have power and vitality available, but you need to be sure that you are putting all that energy into positive directions. This is the best time of the month for putting carefully thought-out plans into operation, and to gain plenty of support when you need it the most. Money matters should settle.

29 WEDNESDAY   *Moon Age Day 4   Moon Sign Cancer*

Stand by for a hectic spell when getting onside with current news and views can be especially important. Now is the time to organise your personal schedule as carefully as you can and don't crowd yourself out with jobs that are not at all necessary. The middle of this week is fine for making a financial commitment, but think carefully first.

30 THURSDAY   *Moon Age Day 5   Moon Sign Cancer*

You can gain from discussing ideas with other people and should be at your mental best under present planetary trends. Even if it seems to take you ages to finish something left over from the past, once you have it out of the way the horizon ahead looks clear. Romance could be on the mind of many Taurus subjects at this time.

May

2009

1 FRIDAY
Moon Age Day 6   Moon Sign Cancer

There is now a powerful emphasis on money-making, and that isn't too surprising for Taurus, which is a naturally acquisitive sign. A new month brings fresh ideas and for some it might even spell a new job. You can afford to remain active and enterprising and to finish the working week on a real flourish. Popularity is there for the taking.

2 SATURDAY
Moon Age Day 7   Moon Sign Leo

An intimate matter may prove to be rather taxing, creating the feeling that relationships can be more trouble than they are worth. For this reason you might decide to stick to casual attachments and even to people who are acquaintances rather than personal friends. Don't be afraid to change your attitude and show your usual kindness.

3 SUNDAY
Moon Age Day 8   Moon Sign Leo

Some actions can be self-defeating but in the main you have what it takes to move forward solidly towards your chosen objectives. Keep up with what those around you are planning and don't get left behind in the planning stage of journeys or adventures. Your strength lies in remaining generally positive and committed to the future.

4 MONDAY
Moon Age Day 9   Moon Sign Virgo

Being a Taurean you can be a stickler for detail and the present time is no exception in this regard. You may not be willing to let others finalise details for anything you see as being your own prerogative, and could be fussy beyond belief on occasions. You tend to stick to tried and tested methods for getting things done today.

100

5 TUESDAY
Moon Age Day 10   Moon Sign Virgo

An ideal day to strengthen your finances and perhaps identify some cash that you can spend more or less as you wish. That doesn't mean to say you will be throwing money around, and you should remain pretty keen to run your own show. This applies to all aspects of life – business or social.

6 WEDNESDAY
Moon Age Day 11   Moon Sign Libra

Spirits are good, so be prepared to put plenty of effort into getting ahead on the social scene. You love to be in the company of intelligent and interesting people and should have much to contribute when you are. Anything grubby or unsavoury is best avoided at present, and you can afford to leave less favourable jobs to others.

7 THURSDAY
☿   *Moon Age Day 12   Moon Sign Libra*

You can best set the precedent for the day by refusing to be hurried or overconcerned with material worries or irrelevant details. Mars remains in your solar twelfth house and this encourages you to look deep inside yourself in some ways. The deeper and more spiritual side of your nature is inspired by this planetary position.

8 FRIDAY
☿   *Moon Age Day 13   Moon Sign Scorpio*

With the lunar low now present you may decide not to push the boat out in any way today. Many Taurus people may be happy to stay in the background and to get on with jobs that may not be glamorous but which are nevertheless necessary. A few hours in your own company might do you the world of good.

9 SATURDAY
☿   *Moon Age Day 14   Moon Sign Scorpio*

Certain frustrations could arise today, but if you deal with these one at a time and refuse to get yourself into any sort of panic, you can ensure all is well. It's worth persuading friends to lend a helping hand and seeking support from your partner. Slow and steady wins the race – as Taurus knows.

10 SUNDAY ☿ *Moon Age Day 15   Moon Sign Scorpio*

If you, your partner, or both of you require a greater sense of freedom now, that is something you can easily share. You can also achieve commonality of purpose between you and a good friend – so you need not be short of someone to share a potential adventure. All the same you needn't tell the whole world everything today.

11 MONDAY ☿ *Moon Age Day 16   Moon Sign Sagittarius*

You have every opportunity at this stage of the month to address and improve financial matters. Getting things moving in a more positive direction at work is also highlighted, and you have scope to tap into a great deal more energy than has been the case for the last few days at least.

12 TUESDAY ☿ *Moon Age Day 17   Moon Sign Sagittarius*

With the Sun now so firmly placed in your solar first house and with the lunar low now right out of the way, there is no real obstacle to your potential for success. You have been thinking for some time, and now is the moment to push on. Don't be afraid to seek out people who are in a position to help you and if necessary employ some cheek!

13 WEDNESDAY ☿ *Moon Age Day 18   Moon Sign Capricorn*

Trends promote an itch for excitement and maybe some long-distance travel. If money has been an issue recently, you should be able to improve things significantly. They say that all things come to those who wait and this certainly seems to be the case for you during the next week or two. Your social attitudes may be on the change.

14 THURSDAY ☿ *Moon Age Day 19   Moon Sign Capricorn*

You can be at your most inventive and communicative right now and should have plenty to say for yourself in just about any situation. Some Taureans will be on a push towards better health and a greater sense of strength, and that could mean alternative regimes. Keep up with all forms of communication for the best results today.

15 FRIDAY
☿ *Moon Age Day 20*   *Moon Sign Capricorn*

That twelfth-house Mars is still present and could prove to be the only fly in the ointment when it comes to personal relationships. You may not be quite as secure as you would wish to be and there can be aggravating little niggles in your mind. Try to relax and where possible take things at face value. Beware of getting tied to routines.

16 SATURDAY
☿ *Moon Age Day 21*   *Moon Sign Aquarius*

There is no doubt that you are in the midst of a period that offers tremendous energy and a determination to see things through to their natural conclusion. Wishing to improve your current lot in life is not unusual for Taurus, but the incentives are much stronger under present trends. A good romantic interlude could be on the way.

17 SUNDAY
☿ *Moon Age Day 22*   *Moon Sign Aquarius*

This is a time for heightened imagination and a period during which your natural creativity is much enhanced. For this you can thank little Mercury in your solar first house, where it assists the Sun in encouraging inventiveness. Old ways of dealing with issues can now be swapped for new and revolutionary alternatives.

18 MONDAY
☿   *Moon Age Day 23*   *Moon Sign Pisces*

A much more harmonious phase is now beginning. With the Moon in a favourable position you have what it takes to get on well with almost everyone – even people you didn't take to before. Having fun with friends and colleagues is well starred this week, and you can afford to be at the front of organisations or new social groups.

19 TUESDAY
☿   *Moon Age Day 24*   *Moon Sign Pisces*

Almost certainly you can further your success potential with fresh starts and a very positive frame of mind. There is a rewarding sense of vigour around now, and that ability you have to keep going when others fall by the wayside has never been better than it turns out to be right now. Don't stick fast if decisions have to be made.

20 WEDNESDAY ☿ *Moon Age Day 25 Moon Sign Aries*

Though there may be slightly less progress to be made in the competitive world for the next two or three days, that doesn't mean you should be giving up on anything. However, while the Moon passes through your solar twelfth house you may be more inclined to plan than to act. Emotional attachments are highlighted between now and Friday.

21 THURSDAY ☿ *Moon Age Day 26 Moon Sign Aries*

Planetary trends favour the acquisition of money right now, and even if you have worries about how you will spend cash, getting more of it shouldn't be too much of a problem. The time is right to build on recent triumphs, and though there may be a few frustrations about now, these are minor and won't last long.

22 FRIDAY ☿ *Moon Age Day 27 Moon Sign Aries*

You have only a few hours to wait before the Moon races back into your own zodiac sign, bringing with it probably the most progressive phase for weeks. In the meantime you should be clearing the decks for action that comes later, and may also decide to spend time in the company of those you know are as progressive as you are now.

23 SATURDAY ☿ *Moon Age Day 28 Moon Sign Taurus*

This influence enables you to get on a winning streak. Your intuition is especially well honed at present so you should not distrust that little voice at the back of your mind. Activities of all sorts should appeal to you whilst the lunar high is around, and it looks as though the world will need to be on its toes to keep up with you.

24 SUNDAY ☿ *Moon Age Day 0 Moon Sign Taurus*

The swifter your decisions and actions are today, the better situations should work out for you. You have what it takes to get on well, whilst at the same time being able to put others at their ease. In social settings you can shine like a star, so don't be surprised if people generally want to have you around as much as possible.

25 MONDAY ☿ *Moon Age Day 1* *Moon Sign Gemini*

You may be up against certain limitations when it comes to running your love life in the way you might wish. Alternative approaches are called for and you have a chance to show just how calculating you are capable of being. This isn't necessarily a bad thing. It simply means you know what you want and how to go about getting it.

26 TUESDAY ☿ *Moon Age Day 2* *Moon Sign Gemini*

Now is the time to use your charm to get more or less anything you want from others. That's fine up to a point, but of course you also have to live with your own conscience, which might prick you mightily if you feel you have taken advantage. Don't get too hung up on issues that rightfully belong in the past.

27 WEDNESDAY ☿ *Moon Age Day 3* *Moon Sign Cancer*

This is a good time for getting ahead in monetary and practical issues. There might not be quite as much time or opportunity as you would wish to further your objectives when it comes to love – particularly if the object of your desire is away or otherwise engaged. In almost all settings you can now be relied upon to be sensible.

28 THURSDAY ☿ *Moon Age Day 4* *Moon Sign Cancer*

You can afford to feel fairly relaxed, though you may not be making quite the level of progress that was possible a few days ago. This could be frustrating, but if you stop to think there are ways around almost any situation. In particular you can be quite inventive right now, so can handle old issues in a very new and innovative way.

29 FRIDAY ☿ *Moon Age Day 5* *Moon Sign Leo*

Trends suggest some touchiness and reluctance when dealing with your social life or when called upon to come out with words of love. Maybe people are failing to respond in the way you would wish or else they don't seem to take you very seriously. Not everything is what it seems and it is important now to keep your eyes open.

30 SATURDAY ☿ *Moon Age Day 6 Moon Sign Leo*

Things can change rapidly amongst the planets and it looks as though love is definitely an area worth some more concentration today. The Moon comes to your aid, assisting you to find the right expressions to knock someone off their feet, and you may also discover you have an admirer you never even suspected.

31 SUNDAY ☿ *Moon Age Day 7 Moon Sign Virgo*

While showing great generosity towards others you can also make a stronger and better path for yourself when it comes to planning for the future. Life is a mixture of possibilities at the moment, and like a child in a sweet shop it might sometimes be difficult for you to decide. Never mind, there's no particular rush right now.

June

2009

1 MONDAY
Moon Age Day 8   Moon Sign Virgo

Venus remains in your solar twelfth house, encouraging reticence when it comes to speaking your mind or pushing yourself ahead as much as you have been doing recently. The main area of concern is with regard to love. Even though someone might tell you how important you are, will you believe them?

2 TUESDAY
Moon Age Day 9   Moon Sign Libra

This has potential to be a busy time at work, and you may not have too many spare moments. For this reason you need to be well organised and able to get things right first time. There isn't a better sign of the zodiac than yours for being practical and for letting everyone know that you are quite certain of your ground. Beware of being clingy in love.

3 WEDNESDAY
Moon Age Day 10   Moon Sign Libra

The focus is now on practical work and on your overwhelming desire not to let things slide. Colleagues may be less committed than you are and this could be a slight bone of contention. When work is out of the way you can afford to ring the changes in some way and, if possible, to travel. Holidays will be beckoning for some lucky Taureans.

4 THURSDAY
Moon Age Day 11   Moon Sign Scorpio

Life can have a slightly topsy-turvy feel at the moment, and the lunar low does little to help you make the level of progress you would desire. Arguments are possible at home, even if these are not being inspired by you. It might prove necessary to pour oil on troubled water, and that can take time.

5 FRIDAY
Moon Age Day 12   Moon Sign Scorpio

Any obstacles, delays or frustrations needn't be allowed to hold you up for more than a few minutes. It isn't the intensity of issues that is the problem now but more the fact that they stop the flow of your life. This is a very temporary situation, and one that can have a great deal of humour or even comedy about it.

6 SATURDAY
Moon Age Day 13   Moon Sign Scorpio

You can be alert and even forceful when necessary, which might surprise a few people, particularly if you have been much quieter across the last couple of days. This is a weekend when you can have fun, and a time that demands your attention to do whatever you see as being important. DIY is an option for some Bulls now.

7 SUNDAY
Moon Age Day 14   Moon Sign Sagittarius

There is plenty of mental energy around now, which can be used to complement your physical efforts to make necessary changes. In most situations you can get well ahead of the game, and this turns out to be especially important in the case of Taurus subjects who work at the weekend. It's worth saving some time later to have fun with people you like.

8 MONDAY
Moon Age Day 15   Moon Sign Sagittarius

Now you have scope to show a much more decisive side to your nature. You know very well what you want from life and should have a very good idea how to get it. Bear in mind that any impatience could hinder your ability to deal with the emotional needs of others.

9 TUESDAY
Moon Age Day 16   Moon Sign Capricorn

A day to focus on practical goals and get yourself into the right frame of mind to finish jobs that are left over from a few days ago. When it comes to building financial security you should be at your best, and shouldn't be fazed by small difficulties that come your way. Be prepared to help out a friend in need.

10 WEDNESDAY *Moon Age Day 17   Moon Sign Capricorn*

Social events can now lift your spirits, leaving you feeling rather more contented with your lot than might have been the case at the start of the week. Look out for possible surprises, especially from the direction of your lover or a good friend. Make the most of a strong impulsive streak that is on offer for much of the rest of the week.

11 THURSDAY *Moon Age Day 18   Moon Sign Capricorn*

Trends encourage your lightning wit and sense of fun. Be prepared to capitalise on this in order to attract company and enjoy social events. There is little chance of quiet interludes but if you do get the odd moment alone you will want to make the most of it. Involve family members today.

12 FRIDAY *Moon Age Day 19   Moon Sign Aquarius*

In terms of your career there are signs that you now want to do things your own way. This could cause one or two problems if co-operation with others is necessary, but there are ways and means of getting round this problem if you stop and think. This is not a good day to be too impulsive, and rushing your fences could mean problems arise.

13 SATURDAY *Moon Age Day 20   Moon Sign Aquarius*

Mars is still in your solar first house and, taken together with other planetary trends, this encourages impulsiveness. You tend to act first and ask questions later, which might get you into a few difficult situations. It would be better by far to react to life in the way a steady and thoughtful Taurus person should.

14 SUNDAY *Moon Age Day 21   Moon Sign Pisces*

This particular Sunday should be good for social get-togethers and for chewing the fat with friends and family members alike. With moments to spare you can also afford to give more attention to your partner and to make a fuss of them at every opportunity. A small gift or a special favour could work wonders!

15 MONDAY
Moon Age Day 22   Moon Sign Pisces

If you use your communication skills you can get what you want simply by asking for it. There should be absolutely no need to throw your weight about. Be prepared to articulate yourself very well indeed and to find new ways to express old ideas. Approach all objectives in the absolute expectation that you will succeed.

16 TUESDAY
Moon Age Day 23   Moon Sign Pisces

The Moon in your solar twelfth house today and tomorrow offers an introspective time when you may not be too anxious to push yourself forward in the way you have been doing recently. You do presently have the ability to solve complex problems, and needn't let yourself be beaten by any sort of puzzle.

17 WEDNESDAY
Moon Age Day 24   Moon Sign Aries

The introspective interlude continues, offering you a chance to sort out issues from the past. As the day advances you can start to notch up little successes and should be quite keen to demonstrate your capabilities in a fairly modest way. Venus in your first house assists you to be very romantic.

18 THURSDAY
Moon Age Day 25   Moon Sign Aries

This has potential to be a good day for sorting out business matters and for getting to grips with issues that could have stumped you in the past. Any sort of financial matter can be dealt with easily and you can persuade people not to argue with your opinions in the main. You might not find excitement until tomorrow, but stability is important too.

19 FRIDAY
Moon Age Day 26   Moon Sign Taurus

It's a good time to start something new. The lunar high offers more energy and better ideas. Put your creative ideas to practical use and start the social side of the weekend as soon as you can this evening. You can afford to remain deeply romantic and very committed to showing your lover just how important they are to your life in general.

20 SATURDAY *Moon Age Day 27   Moon Sign Taurus*

You can quite easily gain the help and admiration of most people today and needn't be short of admirers. Success is there for the taking in almost anything you decide to undertake, and you can make the most of your general popularity. Perhaps best of all you are lucky in a financial sense and can take the odd chance.

21 SUNDAY *Moon Age Day 28   Moon Sign Gemini*

The lunar high moves away and leaves in its wake a tendency for you to be rather more optimistic than some situations deserve. Still, a positive attitude can enable you to move forward nearly as much as fantastic good luck. A few people could annoy you today, especially if they are loud or brash. You prefer demur and cultured.

22 MONDAY *Moon Age Day 29   Moon Sign Gemini*

You now have an excellent opportunity to be a 'people person'. You have what it takes to get on well with almost everyone and can easily change and adapt your nature to suit the circumstances. This stands you in good stead at work, or wherever you are surrounded by others. Taurus is now at it brightest and most social best.

23 TUESDAY *Moon Age Day 0   Moon Sign Cancer*

Fresh experiences could well appeal to you at this time and you may not take kindly to being stuck in any sort of rut. It's worth fighting tenaciously in order to have fresh air to breath, and new horizons to view. This applies just as much at work as it does in a social sense, and some Taureans may even be thinking about changing jobs soon.

24 WEDNESDAY *Moon Age Day 1   Moon Sign Cancer*

There seems to be a very assertive phase on offer – a time when you won't second-guess anything but will be keen to know all details yourself. That means you might be extremely careful and even quite pedantic at times. Even if this seems quite natural to you, it might cause raised eyebrows from others. That's their problem!

25 THURSDAY
Moon Age Day 2   Moon Sign Leo

Fortunate dealings with the world at large are indicated, and you have scope to remain very sociable and warm. Of course it might be suggested that you are like this most of the time, but there is a quieter side to Taurus that isn't on display just now. At work your strength lies in searching for answers and following all new leads.

26 FRIDAY
Moon Age Day 3   Moon Sign Leo

You can gain a great deal now if you are willing to share your innermost feelings with those around you. A journey down memory lane may be fun, but it probably won't help you when it comes to making decisions for the here and now. As long as you are realistic in your view of the past all should be well, but don't remain there too long.

27 SATURDAY
Moon Age Day 4   Moon Sign Virgo

Today assists you to bring out the fun side of your personality and show your best face to the world at large. This really does qualify as a key day, simply because you can get everything to line up in the way you would wish. Relationships can be particularly secure, and you can afford to make extra efforts to please family and friends.

28 SUNDAY
Moon Age Day 5   Moon Sign Virgo

Venus is still in your solar first house – which is where it definitely should be in the case of the zodiac sign of Taurus. This allows you to make relationships more secure and to offer the very best of your cultured nature to the world at large. It's worth keeping abreast of current news and views in the area where you live and getting involved.

29 MONDAY
Moon Age Day 6   Moon Sign Libra

Your emotions could now be slightly erratic because there are different forces at work within your nature. Venus is alongside Mars in your solar first house and this is what supports the slight emotional seesaws that are possible. Even if you feel settled and secure, there may be an underlying restlessness you can't really identify.

30 TUESDAY   *Moon Age Day 7   Moon Sign Libra*

A day to concentrate your energies on being productive and to take time out to solicit help from others when you need it the most. If you've been handing out favours across the last few weeks, you shouldn't have any difficulty getting colleagues and friends to rally when you need them. Don't be afraid to seek out something you want.

8
July
2009

1 WEDNESDAY
Moon Age Day 8   Moon Sign Libra

With the lunar low just around the corner you may find that energy levels are dropping away, especially later on today. A two-day period is at hand which encourages you to stop pushing so hard and to take some rest. You can do yourself more good by watching and waiting for a while than you can by constantly pushing on.

2 THURSDAY
Moon Age Day 9   Moon Sign Scorpio

Why not put certain plans on ice and settle for a quite and reflective sort of day? You have what it takes to persuade others to take the strain whilst you recharge flagging batteries and spend at least some time on your own. Things that have now fully run their course need to be abandoned and there are moments of true reflection on offer.

3 FRIDAY
Moon Age Day 10   Moon Sign Scorpio

Even if you start today quietly, that needn't be the way things are in the longer term. On the contrary, that first-house Mars encourages you forward again and ensures that a temporary holiday from responsibilities and effort has come to an end. You probably won't be sorry to be back in gear.

4 SATURDAY
Moon Age Day 11   Moon Sign Sagittarius

Information that you can glean today could prove to be invaluable. You have potential to be a skilled diplomat and negotiator and can easily help others to come to agreements, even when this seems most unlikely. It's a pity you are not in charge of foreign policy. If you were, there would never be any wars!

5 SUNDAY
Moon Age Day 12   Moon Sign Sagittarius

You have scope to put yourself in the limelight today, and without really trying very hard. If you can remain attractive and approachable, you can get almost everyone to be your friend and to work hard to please you. Of course there are going to be those who see things differently, but that shouldn't bother you too much.

6 MONDAY
Moon Age Day 13   Moon Sign Sagittarius

Be prepared to get out and enjoy what nature has to offer this week. There is no point at all in being stuck indoors and you have scope to enjoy life much better if you are getting some fresh air and a change of scenery. Your imagination is well starred, and this should stand you in good stead both at work and later when you are relaxing.

7 TUESDAY
Moon Age Day 14   Moon Sign Capricorn

You have so much drive and 'oomph' available at the moment it is just possible that some people will find the situation somewhat threatening. Of course this isn't your intention, but then you can't make allowances for everyone. Simply be yourself and do things in your own way. At least you can impress those who know you well with your enthusiasm.

8 WEDNESDAY
Moon Age Day 15   Moon Sign Capricorn

This has potential to be an excellent phase for gathering information. It's important today to listen to what everyone has to say, whether you know them well or not. Even the most casual of remarks can help you to think in new ways, and there ought to be plenty of opportunities to impress superiors and those who have influence.

9 THURSDAY
Moon Age Day 16   Moon Sign Aquarius

You could encounter a few challenging issues today, but you can use these to discover positive things about yourself that you did not know. This puts you in the good position to keep moving ahead progressively and to get at least some of what you want from life. You can persuade friends to be both compliant and charming now.

10 FRIDAY
Moon Age Day 17   Moon Sign Aquarius

The focus is on your energy and strength at this time. There are some very powerful supporting influences around, many of which have a bearing on your business life. From a social point of view you have scope to be with like-minded people and to enjoy the cut and thrust of lively debate.

11 SATURDAY
Moon Age Day 18   Moon Sign Aquarius

You can use your vitality and charm to gain popularity with all sorts of people, and present trends open up the possibility of a very enjoyable weekend. This is the best time imaginable for social activities and for enjoying the warmth of summer. Being forced to remain in the same place for any length of time will probably not appeal.

12 SUNDAY
Moon Age Day 19   Moon Sign Pisces

It would be sensible to be careful with money for the next day or two. It isn't that you are likely to be on the receiving end of bad luck, merely that you will do better, pound for pound, if you hold onto cash for a few days. Today is ideal for contacting friends you don't see very often, and for taking a journey of some sort.

13 MONDAY
Moon Age Day 20   Moon Sign Pisces

Both financially and in terms of work you are now driven to manage and control situations. This is because Mars has now entered your solar second house. Gone are the slight problems this planet has caused you for the last few months, replaced by a much more positive and useful phase that allows you to be more or less fully in command.

14 TUESDAY
Moon Age Day 21   Moon Sign Aries

Many planets are moving around in your chart now and one really positive alteration is the movement of Mercury into your solar third house. This assists with communications of all kinds and is especially useful in helping you to explain yourself to colleagues. There can be great wisdom in what you are saying at present.

15 WEDNESDAY   *Moon Age Day 22   Moon Sign Aries*

Put your persuasive tongue to work today and be willing to speak out when you sense the time is right. You can afford to rely on your intuition, which remains particularly strong at the moment. Attitude is now very important when you are forced to confront issues you have been trying to avoid. You will be amazed at your success!

16 THURSDAY   *Moon Age Day 23   Moon Sign Taurus*

With your instincts honed to perfection and with the lunar high helping you out, it looks as though the sky is the limit. You can make this the most positive period of the month, and though it demands a great deal in the way of energy, the results should be more than worthwhile. In company you simply need to be what you naturally are.

17 FRIDAY   *Moon Age Day 24   Moon Sign Taurus*

This would be an excellent time either to start a new job or to go on a journey. Either way you can be in command of your own life, and even if nothing special seems to be happening it will be worth paying attention to the nuances of life. You can attract support from people and directions you never even expected.

18 SATURDAY   *Moon Age Day 25   Moon Sign Taurus*

As today begins the Moon still occupies your own zodiac sign of Taurus. That should help you to give extra impetus to the weekend and set you off in the right direction when it comes to decisions you have to make. Don't be afraid to vary routines as much as possible – or else ignore them altogether. What you need now is variety in truckloads.

19 SUNDAY   *Moon Age Day 26   Moon Sign Gemini*

Your powers of attraction have rarely been better. That's fine if you are looking for a new relationship, but can be a little embarrassing if you are not. It's okay for people to like you, but their reactions can also be a cause of slight jealousy on the part of your partner. Just stay as charming as you are and you can sort everything out.

20 MONDAY
Moon Age Day 27   Moon Sign Gemini

Today mainly centres on communications with the outside world. With the Sun in your solar third house at the moment, you still have what it takes to make a firm and positive impression, simply by opening your mouth. Not everyone wants to agree with you, but some could be finding it increasingly difficult to avoid doing so.

21 TUESDAY
Moon Age Day 28   Moon Sign Cancer

The tendency to potential boredom seems quite strong for the moment and you would be wise to do everything in your power to vary routines and to keep yourself busy throughout today. As long as you get enough variety into your life you can shrug off a tendency to get frustrated with others. By tomorrow you can make sure things look different.

22 WEDNESDAY
Moon Age Day 0   Moon Sign Cancer

Trends encourage you to focus a good deal today on property and possessions. This isn't particularly unusual for Taurus and you can sometimes be quite acquisitive. New plans put into practice now can mean greater gains further down the road, and you can be in a very organisational frame of mind. Why not seek support from friends?

23 THURSDAY
Moon Age Day 1   Moon Sign Leo

The Sun now moves into your solar fourth house, which is always a good sign for the Bull. This position of the Sun allows you to be much closer to family members and more romantic and caring. You have what it takes to get people interested in cultivating your acquaintance and to make progress in work-related matters.

24 FRIDAY
Moon Age Day 2   Moon Sign Leo

It is increasingly towards home and family that you are now encouraged to turn your attention. It could be that you are in the middle of major changes or you might simply be wanting to tweak domestic situations to make them more comfortable. Whatever you decide to, there's much to be said for being a home-bird now.

25 SATURDAY   *Moon Age Day 3   Moon Sign Virgo*

Romance can be given a definite boost and you can put yourself firmly in the limelight socially. The weekend offers more in the way of new delights – some of which might come courtesy of your partner or close family members. You have scope to get everyone to do what they can to make you both happy and comfortable.

26 SUNDAY   *Moon Age Day 4   Moon Sign Virgo*

Even if you are still in the market for making money, chances are that you might be parting with some too. If things seem to be more expensive than they were, ask yourself whether you are getting the best value possible. It's worth doing a little comparing before you part with any more cash.

27 MONDAY   *Moon Age Day 5   Moon Sign Libra*

You will be better suited to solo pursuits at the start of this particular week, mainly because of a sense that if you want to get anything done properly it would be best to do it yourself. The attitude of colleagues could be awkward or surprising, and you might even fall out with people who just can't seem to get it together somehow.

28 TUESDAY   *Moon Age Day 6   Moon Sign Libra*

A day to avoid confrontations by staying on your own and to continue to plough your own furrow whenever possible. This probably isn't the most progressive time of the month, and with the lunar low just around the corner you will need your reserves of energy and patience. Stick to social matters when you can because they are more settled.

29 WEDNESDAY   *Moon Age Day 7   Moon Sign Scorpio*

Success may be only modest for the next couple of days and you might be best off clearing the decks for action that will come a little later. Don't be too quick to take offence if things don't seem to be going your way, and avoid reacting harshly to more or less unimportant situations. Your strength lies in your ability to laugh at yourself.

30 THURSDAY   *Moon Age Day 8   Moon Sign Scorpio*

If a critical decision leaves you in two minds, the best way forward would be to seek the advice of an impartial friend. At the same time you can afford to support others, though you may not have the necessary reserves of energy when you need them the most. By tomorrow you can make sure things are less stressed.

31 FRIDAY   *Moon Age Day 9   Moon Sign Sagittarius*

Your business ideas and initiatives can now be given more support and it is important for you to get back on form. With greater patience and a genuine desire to be of help you can repair any little cracks that have appeared in personal relationships, whilst at the same time cultivating new friends and getting involved in brand new social activities.

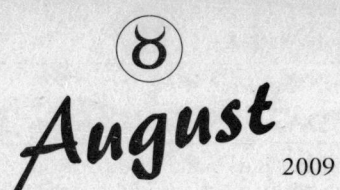

August 2009

1 SATURDAY
Moon Age Day 10   Moon Sign Sagittarius

On the ideas level you have scope to benefit from new input and from the involvement of people in your life who have not played an important part before. You may decide to catch up on correspondence or do some shopping. You have good social graces and will relish the company of people you find interesting and intelligent.

2 SUNDAY
Moon Age Day 11   Moon Sign Sagittarius

Your idealism is now extremely powerful and Mars in your solar second house makes you a born natural when it comes to supporting people you consider to have been wronged in any way. That natural Taurean courage can now be put on display and you can afford to fight tenaciously on behalf of causes in which you wholeheartedly believe.

3 MONDAY
Moon Age Day 12   Moon Sign Capricorn

Though this is definitely a period during which you can bring out the best in others, something in your own life might seem to be lacking. Why not find the time early this week to look around and decide what it is that you most want to do? Having decided, all that remains is to put your mind to finding ways to get things moving.

4 TUESDAY
Moon Age Day 13   Moon Sign Capricorn

With the Sun still so strong in your solar fourth house there is little doubt that the first two-thirds of this month are going to be heavily biased in favour of those you love the most. Now is the time to seek rewarding moments at home, and to take pride in younger family members.

121

5 WEDNESDAY   *Moon Age Day 14   Moon Sign Aquarius*

Even if there are demands being made on your time and energy, you can still manage to fit more into your days than most people do. Deep inside you may be a longing for quiet spaces and time to spend on your own, but current trends may not help you to achieve this. Money matters could be variable.

6 THURSDAY   *Moon Age Day 15   Moon Sign Aquarius*

Don't be afraid to seek tangible and practical support from those higher up the tree than you. You should now be able to get on top of money concerns and will be somewhat wiser in the way you are parting with cash. Be prepared to lift other sorts of weights from your mind around now.

7 FRIDAY   *Moon Age Day 16   Moon Sign Aquarius*

The present position of Venus in your chart offers you scope to find exactly the right words to express your love and devotion. A little extra courage may be necessary in order for you to face some sort of practical situation you might have been dreading, but this should turn out to be far less traumatising than you thought.

8 SATURDAY   *Moon Age Day 17   Moon Sign Pisces*

Your social instincts remain strong, assisting you to mix freely with both family and friends, all at the same time. Any sort of function that puts you on the top table will appeal at present, and you can afford to dress up and show off at the drop of a hat. Your confidence could get a boost from an unexpected direction.

9 SUNDAY   *Moon Age Day 18   Moon Sign Pisces*

As far as a few practicalities are concerned your life may now be in the slow lane, but all this does is to give you more time to concentrate on the less tangible but very enjoyable aspects. Make the most of the social side of your nature by mixing freely with many different sorts of people. Confidence to do the right thing is never far away.

10 MONDAY *Moon Age Day 19   Moon Sign Aries*

With the present position of the Moon this would be a good day for winding down certain interests ahead of beginning new ones. You should feel better able to move on properly if you have sorted other things out first. This applies just as much to social matters as it does to anything associated with your work.

11 TUESDAY *Moon Age Day 20   Moon Sign Aries*

You have what it takes to be the centre of attention today and to do everything you can to make yourself noticed. Mercury is moving on rapidly through your chart and at the moment occupies your solar fifth house. Romantic matters are well starred, and your strength lies in getting others to see you in a positive light.

12 WEDNESDAY *Moon Age Day 21   Moon Sign Aries*

This has potential to be another fairly positive day, with plenty for you to crow about and an optimistic feel to almost everything. One of the things that will probably set this week apart is how fresh and new everything feels. Make the most of the summer weather, and if it proves to be possible you might decide to take a day or two off work.

13 THURSDAY *Moon Age Day 22   Moon Sign Taurus*

Matters should be turning out rather well. The lunar high is present, helping you to get pretty much your way. Your buoyant and cheerful personality can be a tonic to just about anyone you meet and as a result your popularity should be going off the scale. Luck is never far away from new initiatives at the moment, so why not get cracking and have a try?

14 FRIDAY *Moon Age Day 23   Moon Sign Taurus*

Don't be afraid to take the odd gamble at the moment and indulge in a few life-changing decisions. You could do worse than to spread your wings in some way. Some Taureans may decide to pursue alterations in employment status and possible changes of career. This is potentially a very positive and happy time.

15 SATURDAY   *Moon Age Day 24   Moon Sign Gemini*

You are entering a period that is going to be very good for any form of constructive change. Present trends may promote a desire for change at home and a need to make alterations to almost anything. Your best response to any restlessness is to settle down and make sure you get all the details right.

16 SUNDAY   *Moon Age Day 25   Moon Sign Gemini*

Now is the time to show others how charming you can be – as if they didn't already know! You can turn this to your advantage, and if there was ever a time for asking for something you really want, this is it. A busy time lies before you but that needn't worry you too much, as long as you keep your level of energy and enthusiasm high.

17 MONDAY   *Moon Age Day 26   Moon Sign Cancer*

On the ideas front you can benefit from new input and it is definitely worthwhile listening to what others have to say today. Even if you don't accept everything they are saying, existing plans and strategies can be altered to suit your own needs and you should be a good team player right now. Confidence is once again on the increase.

18 TUESDAY   *Moon Age Day 27   Moon Sign Cancer*

Be prepared to relax today and wherever possible take care of matters that need sorting out at home. You might not be able to do everything you would wish to change situations, but you can at least put new strategies into action. Many Taureans will be in a party mood at present and it might be good to plan a gathering of some sort.

19 WEDNESDAY   *Moon Age Day 28   Moon Sign Leo*

A get-up-and-go attitude proves best in practical matters. This isn't a good time for waiting to see what will happen, today works best for you when you act. A crucial period is at hand when it comes to negotiating career matters, and though it could seem for a while that you are struggling, you can make sure this isn't the case.

20 THURSDAY
Moon Age Day 0   Moon Sign Leo

The present position of Mercury can be a definite tonic as far as your love life is concerned, so it's worth seeking happiness in relationships. Stay in good company as much as proves to be possible because whether you are at work or at home you relish being with individuals you see as being both intelligent and maybe a little odd.

21 FRIDAY
Moon Age Day 1   Moon Sign Virgo

For another day or two the Sun remains in your solar fourth house, which has made the last month or so even more important as far as domestic matters are concerned. This trend continues in the main, but you could find that you are gradually becoming more restless and that you need more stimulus than your home on its own provides.

22 SATURDAY
Moon Age Day 2   Moon Sign Virgo

Financial matters might need a little more caution now and you would be well advised to keep cash in reserve for situations you didn't expect. Acting on impulse is not to be recommended, and you will be better off using that deep Taurean common sense whenever possible. If family members have other ideas, be prepared to curb them!

23 SUNDAY
Moon Age Day 3   Moon Sign Libra

You have scope to make this a very positive time in terms of relationships, but with the Sun moving on in your chart you may decide to take your lover or family members out of home-based situations and into something quite different. Does this spell holidays? It's possible, and now would certainly be an advantageous time to get away.

24 MONDAY
Moon Age Day 4   Moon Sign Libra

Along comes a new series of influences and the chance of an even more successful time in one-to-one relationships. The focus moves away from family, though there is no need to lessen your commitment to specific individuals. You can use your huge personality to inspire almost anyone.

25 TUESDAY   *Moon Age Day 5   Moon Sign Scorpio*

Energy may now be thin on the ground and the lunar low could take the wind out of your sails far more than you might expect. What will be the results? Well, you could find that you lack energy and that you have to keep doing the same old job time and again. Planetary trends are telling you it's time to take a rest.

26 WEDNESDAY   *Moon Age Day 6   Moon Sign Scorpio*

If responsibilities suddenly seem heavier to carry, it's worth turning to family, friends or colleagues to lend a hand. You do plenty of things for everyone as a rule and nobody will mind helping you out now. The same relates to any worries you may have. They say a problem shared is a problem halved and that can be very true.

27 THURSDAY   *Moon Age Day 7   Moon Sign Scorpio*

Now the lunar low starts to move away. Your best approach is to remain as cool as a cucumber, even if everyone around you is falling to pieces. Taking the initiative should be easy again and you needn't wait for invitations before wading in and getting involved. Creature comforts may now be less important than they were yesterday.

28 FRIDAY   *Moon Age Day 8   Moon Sign Sagittarius*

If standard responses don't work well today, why not think up new ways to have your say? People expect a great deal of you and it is unlikely that you will let anyone down. Confidence remains high to do the right thing by both colleagues and friends, and you can show yourself to be a faithful and reliable companion all round.

29 SATURDAY   *Moon Age Day 9   Moon Sign Sagittarius*

Positive highlights are available as far as your domestic and family life is concerned. This is a time to concentrate specifically on home and property, though this could be a flash in the pan if at the moment it is matters beyond your own doorstep that really count. Beware of getting bogged down with unnecessary and tedious details.

30 SUNDAY   *Moon Age Day 10   Moon Sign Capricorn*

You can afford to turn your attention to the great outdoors in one way or another today. The Moon is in your solar ninth house and it urges you to walk under broad skies and maybe to enjoy what remains of the summer weather. Friends might have plenty to offer you at the moment, and it is worth listening to some of the plans they are hatching.

31 MONDAY   *Moon Age Day 11   Moon Sign Capricorn*

Beware of being too outspoken at the start of this particular week. If you have too much to say for yourself now, you may have to back up your comments later and that could prove to be rather difficult. The more modest you remain, the easier it will be to follow through. Group matters are also highlighted at present.

September
2009

1 TUESDAY
Moon Age Day 12   Moon Sign Capricorn

A new month brings trends that highlight your career and the importance it has to your life as a whole. If there has been something specific at the back of your mind, now is the time to get it out into the open. A newer and a more dynamic attitude can be employed, but this might take a day or two to filter through to your ultimate actions.

2 WEDNESDAY
Moon Age Day 13   Moon Sign Aquarius

This could prove to be one of the best days of the month for either family gatherings or celebrations of one sort or another. A simple and straightforward approach works best when it comes to asking for anything, and it's worth avoiding get-rich-quick schemes that look good on paper but which could turn out to be some sort of nightmare.

3 THURSDAY
Moon Age Day 14   Moon Sign Aquarius

There is a lot of energy available, but not all of it is being concentrated in specific or useful directions. The vibes you give out just now couold make you seem like an explosion in a mattress factory, and friends might have difficulty keeping up with you. Watch, listen and wait. The more meditation you manage now, the better life will be.

4 FRIDAY
Moon Age Day 15   Moon Sign Pisces

The time is right to capitalise on your group-conscious qualities, and as the month advances you can use them to rise to the top of any co-operative venture in which you take part. Being involved should be second nature, but at the same time you may not be especially competitive right now. Taurus is complex, and especially so today.

5 SATURDAY
Moon Age Day 16   Moon Sign Pisces

Make the most of current opportunities for friendship and social activities. This is a weekend that you can make your own, and any routines that might get in the way are best shelved for later. Why not give yourself a real break and enjoy what a wonderful and colourful world has to offer? That means getting out to view it!

6 SUNDAY
Moon Age Day 17   Moon Sign Pisces

Sacrificing your own needs in order to help others is not at all unusual for Taurus but there are ways and means today in which you can support those around you, whilst having a really good time yourself. All in all this is an ideal opportunity to get out and go somewhere. What matters is getting away.

7 MONDAY
☿   *Moon Age Day 18   Moon Sign Aries*

In a professional sense you can take advantage of greater freedom now and should be able to choose your path forward much more readily than has been the case recently. There may also be more opportunities for travel and the chance to spread your wings generally. All in all you can make sure this is an entertaining week.

8 TUESDAY
☿   *Moon Age Day 19   Moon Sign Aries*

Even if it appears that one or two things are presently on hold, today does give you the chance to get things in place for the lunar high, which is just around the corner. The attitudes of some friends might surprise or even shock you, but once you have had time to think things through you can come to terms with their views.

9 WEDNESDAY
☿   *Moon Age Day 20   Moon Sign Taurus*

You have what it takes to get yourself very much on target as far as your goals and ambitions are concerned. You can afford to put a great deal of faith in your natural luck for today and tomorrow, and can use it to get ahead of the crowd, either at work or socially. What really helps you to win out now is your natural optimism.

10 THURSDAY ☿ *Moon Age Day 21   Moon Sign Taurus*

This is another red-letter day for most Bulls and a time when you have scope to fire on all cylinders. Even if others fall by the wayside regarding new plans and altered situations, you can show yourself to be flexible and happy to co-operate. All of this helps you to get yourself noticed and to stock up potential gains for later.

11 FRIDAY ☿ *Moon Age Day 22   Moon Sign Gemini*

It might seem that you are too attached to the past today, particularly if you are paying a lot of attention to the attitudes you had and the actions you took at some stage previously. Rather than being strictly nostalgic, by all means learn from the past. This helps you to avoid making the same mistakes again.

12 SATURDAY ☿ *Moon Age Day 23   Moon Sign Gemini*

This is the time of the month when you would be wise to keep a close eye on your budget. There is a chance you will be overspending and also putting too much reliance on the possibility that something will turn up. This is not at all like careful Taurus, and your best response is to get back to your more usual conservative attitude.

13 SUNDAY ☿ *Moon Age Day 24   Moon Sign Cancer*

A day to capitalise on positive attention that you have been able to attract recently. Today will be favourable for romantic opportunities and for getting on especially well in group situations. You might not be leading the field when you are in company but can still make the most positive impression of all.

14 MONDAY ☿ *Moon Age Day 25   Moon Sign Cancer*

Whilst you can now easily create a stimulating social atmosphere, trends suggest that in some situations you may be rather too outspoken for your own good. Like your present tendency to overspend, this runs contrary to your usual nature. It isn't quite time to slam on the brakes but a lower gear might be in order for a day or two.

15 TUESDAY ☿ *Moon Age Day 26   Moon Sign Leo*

With the Moon presently in your solar fourth house it might seem (even to you) that the time is right to slow down daily activities just a little. You could be expecting rather too much of yourself, and might be better spending more time concentrating specifically on one or two matters, rather than trying to sort out the whole world.

16 WEDNESDAY ☿ *Moon Age Day 27   Moon Sign Leo*

Contentment is possible if you can get domestic matters and family relationships running smoothly. You can afford to go on a journey into the past and look again at the way situations panned out for you. It is fine to be nostalgic now and again. What matters is not allowing what went before to totally govern your life now.

17 THURSDAY ☿ *Moon Age Day 28   Moon Sign Virgo*

Mercury has now moved into your solar sixth house, and that can be a tonic for career developments. It also encourages deep discussions, even with people you hardly know at all. They say a stranger is simply a friend you haven't met yet, and today could allow you to prove this.

18 FRIDAY ☿ *Moon Age Day 29   Moon Sign Virgo*

You still make a very convincing talker and will have the ability to make a significant impact on just about anyone who crosses your path. It's worth extending this far beyond the career world and into your social and romantic life. Taurus individuals who have been looking for a new love to enter their life would be wise to concentrate today.

19 SATURDAY ☿ *Moon Age Day 0   Moon Sign Virgo*

Your thirst for knowledge is now emphasised, and the needs of those requiring your help may fade in importance. Look around yourself and take note of those who are struggling. It won't always be too convenient to lend a hand, but you will kick yourself later if you don't.

20 SUNDAY ☿ *Moon Age Day 1   Moon Sign Libra*

Venus is now also in your solar fourth house, as is Mercury. All in all this makes for a very domestic interlude that shows just how important home and family can be to you. There's much to be said for counting your blessings and doing all you can to make things comfortable for the people you love.

21 MONDAY ☿ *Moon Age Day 2   Moon Sign Libra*

This working week may not run quite as smoothly as you might wish, but it all really depends on the way you start out. Tomorrow and Wednesday will encourage you to slow down and there will be no getting away from the fact that your energy levels will be low. If you bear that in mind today, you should be able to work things out.

22 TUESDAY ☿ *Moon Age Day 3   Moon Sign Scorpio*

Certain projects and ideas might have to wait. Trying to keep up with everything could lead to you making mistakes and tiring yourself into the bargain. Don't be afraid to stand back and watch others for a while. If they make a few small mistakes you can put matters right later. You need to slow down and contemplate life a little.

23 WEDNESDAY ☿ *Moon Age Day 4   Moon Sign Scorpio*

The lunar low is still around and it can be quite potent this month. If you insist on pushing on as normal it could feel as though you are carrying the weight of the world on your back. On the other hand, if you seek help and take things steady you could sail through today and hardly notice that anything is much different.

24 THURSDAY ☿ *Moon Age Day 5   Moon Sign Sagittarius*

Now is the time to pick up the pace and get yourself back in the thick of situations. Today offers a chance to stimulate your brain cells with puzzles and mysteries of one sort or another. You want answers to questions and in your present state of mind you should know where to find them.

25 FRIDAY ☿ *Moon Age Day 6   Moon Sign Sagittarius*

This is a time of the month when romance is definitely well starred. Whether you are 16 or 60, Cupid could come knocking on your door at any moment. You will want to be ready and should not be too surprised if you discover that you are flavour of the month. You don't seem to do anything – it simply happens!

26 SATURDAY ☿ *Moon Age Day 7   Moon Sign Capricorn*

Be prepared to keep life stimulating and interesting. The weekend offers a variety of possibilities and all you have to do is to make yourself available for them. Any form of travel may also fascinate you and a late holiday would suit you well. Under present trends you need to be well aware of the favours that you can obtain from friends.

27 SUNDAY ☿ *Moon Age Day 8   Moon Sign Capricorn*

The scope for planning ahead and getting your own way is now especially good. Instead of just reacting to circumstances as they come along, now is the time for you to make the running and to sort your life out very deliberately. The coming week brings new incentives and you will want to be ready to make the most of them.

28 MONDAY ☿ *Moon Age Day 9   Moon Sign Capricorn*

Be careful because there could be verbal outbursts from others today that have potential to take you by surprise. You too could be rather too impulsive for your own good and arguments will follow if you try to bulldoze your ideas, rather than discussing them sensibly. Routines may not interest you at all at this time.

29 TUESDAY ☿ *Moon Age Day 10   Moon Sign Aquarius*

Personal relationships and romance are in the frame again, and with Mercury and Venus now both entering your solar fifth house, today is ideal for getting out there amongst the crowds and soaking up the attention you can attract. You don't really have to do much to be popular – it's something that simply happens now.

30 WEDNESDAY ☿ *Moon Age Day 11   Moon Sign Aquarius*

In a work sense you can now make the most of successes that are coming about as a result of the effort you put in before. If you took the risks and did that extra bit of work, it's only right you should receive the rewards. You can also get a great deal of assistance in your endeavours at present, simply by asking for it.

October

2009

1 THURSDAY
Moon Age Day 12   Moon Sign Pisces

You have scope to make almost any sort of encounter with others on the first day of this month both rewarding and entertaining. You tend to be a fairly social animal under most circumstances but rarely to a greater extent than turns out to be the case at the moment. There are significant opportunities about to mix business with pleasure.

2 FRIDAY
Moon Age Day 13   Moon Sign Pisces

With a little more money at your disposal, trends encourage you to get out there and spend more. This is not universally the case for Taurus, which can even be miserly on occasions. Communication skills remain good and you shouldn't have any trouble getting onside with people you may have found to be awkward before.

3 SATURDAY
Moon Age Day 14   Moon Sign Pisces

You would be wise to avoid potentially deceptive situations and ignore the glib words of those who promise something for nothing. Even if n o one is trying to cheat you, there are a few individuals who are not to be trusted. Your strength lies in realising that in the main you have to work hard for what you get.

4 SUNDAY
Moon Age Day 15   Moon Sign Aries

You can use your generally cheerful attitude to make the most of all social gatherings. You may also be slightly restless and won't want to be stuck at home with the same old weekend routines. Whatever it takes to get you out of yourself, you should find in the end that the effort was more than worthwhile.

5 MONDAY · · · · · · · · · · · · *Moon Age Day 16   Moon Sign Aries*

The emphasis at the moment is on the practical side of life. You may not have as much time for personal enjoyment as you might wish but the important thing is that you are getting things done, and that should please you in the longer term. It's worth pursuing career developments this week.

6 TUESDAY · · · · · · · · · · · · *Moon Age Day 17   Moon Sign Taurus*

The lunar high assists you to feel on top of the world and ready to meet any challenge that comes your way. If life doesn't come up to your expectations, you now have scope to find new opportunities. With better luck on your side you should be able to force issues through and to prove to the world how capable you are.

7 WEDNESDAY · · · · · · · · · · · · *Moon Age Day 18   Moon Sign Taurus*

Don't be afraid to take the odd gamble because you can be extremely astute and capable at the moment. This is no time for standing in the shadows but rather the moment when you should be out there in the mainstream of life. Taurus can be very unconventional just now, but that's probably how you enjoy being.

8 THURSDAY · · · · · · · · · · · · *Moon Age Day 19   Moon Sign Gemini*

The Sun remains in your solar sixth house, which makes this potentially one of the best days of the month as far as work is concerned. Once the responsibilities of the day are done with, why not find new ways to have fun? There are gains to be made in almost any situation that sees you mixing with new and interesting people.

9 FRIDAY · · · · · · · · · · · · *Moon Age Day 20   Moon Sign Gemini*

The emphasis remains on fun and on you being able to show others that you are willing to join in and be part of the group. There are times when Taurus is more than happy to watch and wait, but October simply isn't like that for you. On the contrary, whatever is happening around you – chances are you are inspiring it!

10 SATURDAY   *Moon Age Day 21   Moon Sign Gemini*

Whilst you are now able to communicate and to put forward your point of view in an almost forthright manner, not everyone might respond positively to what you have to say. There is just a small chance you will come across as being over-assertive or even dominant. More sharing is necessary because that offers scope for bigger dividends.

11 SUNDAY   *Moon Age Day 22   Moon Sign Cancer*

There are exciting possibilities in the offing. If you work at the weekend, be prepared to make progress in your career, but if the day is your own you can afford to turn your energy towards having fun. Either way you continue to give every evidence of knowing what you are doing and of being extremely capable.

12 MONDAY   *Moon Age Day 23   Moon Sign Cancer*

For a couple of days domestic matters could be of more importance than they tend to be for most of October. The Moon is passing through your solar fourth house, encouraging nostalgia and an inclination to stick around your home more than you have been doing for a while. Friends could be less than happy today.

13 TUESDAY   *Moon Age Day 24   Moon Sign Leo*

A rather busy phase is indicated at work, but you may decide you are not really up for the challenge today. This is a situation that will change soon enough, but for now you need to feel comfortable and won't be keen to take many risks. You can best combat any feelings of insecurity by turning towards those close to you.

14 WEDNESDAY   *Moon Age Day 25   Moon Sign Leo*

Any professional success is likely to come today from the sort of contacts you are making. Be prepared to come out of the insecure phase that has lasted for a couple of days and start to move ahead. Now is the time to use your verbal skills to persuade others to you to help you out in a big way.

15 THURSDAY *Moon Age Day 26 Moon Sign Virgo*

A day to capitalise on the better fortune and plain good luck that is on offer now. It will be easy for you to make the right sort of decisions and you will be less inclined than ever to hang back when there are gains to be made. On the romantic front you can make the most of an especially good interlude between now and next week.

16 FRIDAY *Moon Age Day 27 Moon Sign Virgo*

You seem to be on a roll at work. Issues here bring valuable highlights and you can keep your inventive mind constantly on the go. There is a sideways look at personal securities around this time, but this tendency needn't prevent you from taking the odd chance or for pushing your luck in your contacts with bosses.

17 SATURDAY *Moon Age Day 28 Moon Sign Libra*

Domestic dealings can prove to be somewhat tense and tempers can be quite short. It might appear as if others are at fault but that probably isn't the case. It takes two to tango, and your best approach is to refuse to become involved. However, that might not be too easy if you feel you are being severely provoked.

18 SUNDAY *Moon Age Day 0 Moon Sign Libra*

You can now ensure that any problems that do come along are short-lived and fairly manageable. It's worth taking some time out to enjoy yourself today. All too soon the dark days of winter will be here and you may wish then that you had seen more of the world beyond your own door.

19 MONDAY *Moon Age Day 1 Moon Sign Scorpio*

Energy levels could well be running lower whilst the lunar low is around, and for that reason you may decide to shelve changes you wanted to make to your life early this week. Even if it seems that others are getting ahead in life quicker than you are, this is only a very temporary matter and can soon be rectified.

20 TUESDAY · Moon Age Day 2 · Moon Sign Scorpio

Patience could be tested by life's little drawbacks, but there is enough planetary support around you now for you to get through or round problems. It's simply that if you are not on top form, taking unnecessary risks is probably not to be recommended. Routines might seem comfortable, and you need security now.

21 WEDNESDAY · Moon Age Day 3 · Moon Sign Sagittarius

Things start to look more positive again and you have scope to get on especially well at work. There are gains to be made in unexpected ways, particularly if you are intuitive. It's those little feelings at the back of your mind that need to be monitored and if you feel a particular action is called for – get on with it!

22 THURSDAY · Moon Age Day 4 · Moon Sign Sagittarius

Money matters need a more cautious approach, and you may not be keen to part with cash as much as has sometimes been the case during October. An ideal time to turn casual aquaintances into something much more, and to find new ways of looking at old situations.

23 FRIDAY · Moon Age Day 5 · Moon Sign Sagittarius

A light and casual approach now works best in your social life as the Sun enters your solar seventh house. It will occupy this position for the next month or so and supports a lighter and even sillier Taurus on occasions. If people generally like what they see, your popularity may be going off the scale in the days ahead.

24 SATURDAY · Moon Age Day 6 · Moon Sign Capricorn

Practical matters discussed with others may stir up some ingenious ideas today. You tend to be quite discriminating and won't settle for second-best in anything. Even if not everyone follows your lead this weekend, the people who matter the most to you should be falling in line and helping to make you feel quite important.

25 SUNDAY
Moon Age Day 7   Moon Sign Capricorn

You benefit from being on the move under present planetary trends and might not be too satisfied with life if you have to stay put or tend to weekend routines. If you do have heavy responsibilitiesdon't be afraid to pass these to someone else – at least for today. Even a few hours away from everyday cares can prove to be very important.

26 MONDAY
Moon Age Day 8   Moon Sign Aquarius

The practicalities of life may well take up much of your time, but you may hear something to your advantage when you are not actually toiling away. There could be a strong feeling at the moment that important times are at hand and you need to be very discriminating when it comes to long-term plans or commitments.

27 TUESDAY
Moon Age Day 9   Moon Sign Aquarius

Although it would be much easier in certain situations to simply defer to others, this might not be the best way forward. Uncomfortable though it may be it looks as though you may have to take command. This will mean giving instructions to people who are not always on your side. A little Taurean courage is called for – and you have that!

28 WEDNESDAY
Moon Age Day 10   Moon Sign Aquarius

Group activities are well starred at the moment, offering you scope to co-operate with anyone who seems to have similar ideas and intentions to your own. A lighter and zanier side begins to show itself to some Bulls, and you could even surprise yourself with a tendency to do things that attract an audience.

29 THURSDAY
Moon Age Day 11   Moon Sign Pisces

Communications of almost every sort are now highlighted. Certain diplomatic efforts on your part should lead to positive results further down the road, and you should be willing to alter your own approach to suit different sorts of people. Keep an eye open for romance, because opportunities are there for the taking.

30 FRIDAY
Moon Age Day 12   Moon Sign Pisces

Trends help you to achieve an inspiring social life and to enlist the support of others and advance your goals through partnerships of one sort or another. There is plenty to be done at the moment, but such is your attitude and your resilience that most jobs can be undertaken in half the time you would normally expect.

31 SATURDAY
Moon Age Day 13   Moon Sign Aries

The Moon now enters your solar twelfth house for a couple of days, encouraging you to withdraw somewhat from the world at large ahead of the lunar high. This may not be too noticeable but it's clear that a quiet and thoughtful weekend would suit you down to the ground. Why not get in touch with people you don't speak to very often?

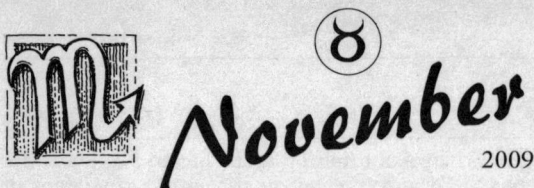 

⑧ November
2009

1 SUNDAY
Moon Age Day 14   Moon Sign Aries

Acts of common kindness and friendliness on your part are not unusual, but you can afford to do more of them now. That's because your empathy is strong and on account of your usual charitable side being much enhanced. Be prepared to offer support and advice to anyone who asks.

2 MONDAY
Moon Age Day 15   Moon Sign Aries

By tomorrow you have potential to be on top form but for the moment keep your powder dry and plan ahead. There are all sorts of possibilities in the offing but circumstances are not yet right for you to act. Dealing with people shouldn't be a problem today, unless their demands are unreasonable.

3 TUESDAY
Moon Age Day 16   Moon Sign Taurus

Although the arrival of the lunar high supports an increase in workload, it is clear that you are up to almost any task and that your level of energy is high. With plenty to keep you occupied, today could pass in a flash, but it's worth saving time later for the strong social possibilities that are on offer. You may also decide to put romance on the agenda.

4 WEDNESDAY
Moon Age Day 17   Moon Sign Taurus

This is a marvellous time in which to be assertive and to make your feelings known. So powerful can be your personality at present that you can use it to make some reasonable requests. Getting what you want from life is only half the picture because you also have scope to make those around you happy too.

142

5 THURSDAY   *Moon Age Day 18   Moon Sign Gemini*

This is one of the best times of the month to reach out and make contacts far beyond the scope of your usual world. Maybe you are busy on the internet, speaking to people who live far away, or it could simply be that your work has a long-distance aspect now. Any form of travel would suit you down to the ground, and change is vital.

6 FRIDAY   *Moon Age Day 19   Moon Sign Gemini*

Trends offer you scope to put yourself at the centre of inspiring discussions. Don't be too keen to take command in all situations because you could find that you are out of your depth in some of them. Be prepared to become second in command if circumstances demand it.

7 SATURDAY   *Moon Age Day 20   Moon Sign Cancer*

An ideal time to channel some of your present energies into changes you want to make in and around your home. You could be putting some sort of pressure on your own personal life, maybe because you are less willing than usual to compromise over issues that really are not that important. Give and take is essential if you are to really enjoy today.

8 SUNDAY   *Moon Age Day 21   Moon Sign Cancer*

Today you can be much more comfortable in personal attachments and should be less inclined than you were to fly off the handle over matters that can be better resolved with patience. You have scope to become a more understanding sort of Bull and to play down that stubborn side that on occasions can typify your Earth-sign nature.

9 MONDAY   *Moon Age Day 22   Moon Sign Leo*

Right now you seem to have the secret of popularity and that is worth a great deal in terms of how well you get on generally. This would be an excellent time to be out socialising, but you can also use these trends to get on very well at work. You should find this to be an excellent way to start the new working week, and there are gains to be made.

10 TUESDAY
Moon Age Day 23   Moon Sign Leo

With the Sun in its present position you have scope to be more outgoing, so now is the time to ask for what you want, instead of waiting and hoping that things will come your way. The spotlight is on communication and sharing, both in business matters and in terms of home and family.

11 WEDNESDAY
Moon Age Day 24   Moon Sign Virgo

The focus for the moment is on exploring and enlarging your personal creativity. Getting things looking good is very important to you at the best of times but especially so just now. You might also decide to show off more in a romantic sense, particularly if you are looking and feeling at your best.

12 THURSDAY
Moon Age Day 25   Moon Sign Virgo

Home and family bring a few challenges, though nothing that need stand in your way for very long. You should be happy enough when mixing with people you have known a long time but could show just a little trepidation if you are expected to deal with newcomers. You may even decide to take refuge in daily routines.

13 FRIDAY
Moon Age Day 26   Moon Sign Libra

This would be the best time of the month to start a new romantic relationship, though of course if you are settled enough with your present partner that isn't going to be an option. All the same there is nothing to prevent you from bringing a little more pep into your love life. Taurus has a good and active imagination, so why not use it now?

14 SATURDAY
Moon Age Day 27   Moon Sign Libra

You could gain significantly from taking a slightly lower profile today. Ahead of the lunar low you can get more out of life by watching and waiting than you can by pitching in too soon or without knowing what is expected of you. Some situations can seem slightly precarious, but things should settle down in two or three days.

15 SUNDAY   *Moon Age Day 28   Moon Sign Scorpio*

It would be a very good idea to take a more relaxed attitude and to watch and wait. Although the lunar low is not very potent this month, silly mistakes are possible if you expect to carry on at your usual speed. Instead of making all the decisions yourself, don't be afraid to defer to family members and friends.

16 MONDAY   *Moon Age Day 29   Moon Sign Scorpio*

As long as you do not try to take too many shortcuts to success at the start of this week, you may not even notice the slightly adverse planetary trends that are surrounding you. Comfort and security are possible, particularly if you avoid pushing yourself or taking part in grandiose schemes.

17 TUESDAY   *Moon Age Day 0   Moon Sign Scorpio*

Your dealings with others offer you scope to enjoy pleasant encounters, and could even be responsible for a friendship that will endure for life. Your love life especially is favoured, and you have what it takes to sweep someone special off their feet. It's worth avoiding unnecessary and tedious chores today.

18 WEDNESDAY   *Moon Age Day 1   Moon Sign Sagittarius*

You interact very well with others at the best of times, but especially so today. Venus remains in your solar seventh house and from that position it helps you to use your charm and be eminently approachable. Once again both friendship and romance can be advanced through your positive attitude, and more personal success is available.

19 THURSDAY   *Moon Age Day 2   Moon Sign Sagittarius*

Trends assist you to be closer to loved ones today and to make your emotional responses deeper and ever more tangible to those you care for. Expressing the way you feel isn't always that easy, but seems to be simple at the present time. As a result you have a chance to glean some equally truthful admissions.

20 FRIDAY
Moon Age Day 3   Moon Sign Capricorn

This has potential to be a freewheeling time and a period when the doors to communication are wide open. You should have no problems at all when it comes to inspiring others to do their best, particularly if you are leading by example. The more you get out and about today, the better you can afford to feel about everything.

21 SATURDAY
Moon Age Day 4   Moon Sign Capricorn

With a little effort on your part you are in a position to clear away old situations and put your mind to what is both new and exciting. Your strength lies in your willingness to put the finishing touches to something that has taken you ages and to be extremely generous in your dealings with others.

22 SUNDAY
Moon Age Day 5   Moon Sign Capricorn

Joint ventures can be well supported by present planetary trends, whether these are of a professional, social or family nature. In a way it doesn't really matter what you decide to do at the moment because you are able to bring the same amount of enthusiasm and determination to bear on it. It's worth paying attention to your love life today.

23 MONDAY
Moon Age Day 6   Moon Sign Aquarius

Trends encourage you to take the lead this week, so why not start today as you mean to go on? That means a sudden if somewhat unexpected rush of energy that might leave others puzzled and dizzy. It might be best to explain yourself before you begin the whirlwind. That way, people are in the picture.

24 TUESDAY
Moon Age Day 7   Moon Sign Aquarius

This is an ideal time for getting rid of things that are not essential to your security or your happiness. Taurus is an Earth sign and can be very sentimental. This can lead to you hanging on to all sorts of objects and ideas that rightfully belong in the dustbin. It's late in the year for spring-cleaning, but it can work wonders all the same.

25 WEDNESDAY   *Moon Age Day 8   Moon Sign Pisces*

The time is right to reshape things, and if you set out with determination you could even surprise yourself. Even if not everyone is on your side today, when the chips are down you can quickly find out who your best supporters are. Don't be too quick to dismiss an idea that might turn out to be a crackerjack in the end.

26 THURSDAY   *Moon Age Day 9   Moon Sign Pisces*

Teamwork and joint efforts are well accented today, assisting you to get on with people – even ones who have caused you a problem or two in the recent past. You have what it takes to gain support from others in social settings, and to persuade colleagues to help you think up new ways to do old tasks.

27 FRIDAY   *Moon Age Day 10   Moon Sign Pisces*

The Sun is now firmly in your solar eighth house, bringing the best period of the year for getting rid of anything that is redundant or out of date. Nostalgia should now play much less of a part in your thinking, and you can afford to be slightiy ruthless in your determination to streamline many aspects of your life.

28 SATURDAY   *Moon Age Day 11   Moon Sign Aries*

As a rule you are famous for being one of the zodiac's plodders, but this needn't be the case at all at the moment. You have scope to tackle almost any problem head-on and can refuse to take no for an answer. People who come from much more dynamic zodiac signs than you do will be taking lessons from your attitude now!

29 SUNDAY   *Moon Age Day 12   Moon Sign Aries*

By tomorrow you can get back on form but with the Moon in your twelfth house today you may decide to settle for quiet times and domestic bliss. You probably won't feel much like travelling far or pushing yourself too hard. There are gains to be made on the domestic scene and it should be possible to reach a new understanding with relatives.

30 MONDAY

Moon Age Day 13   Moon Sign Taurus

This is a day for making the most of sudden possibilities that come along. You shouldn't stick fast and have the ability to act quickly and decisively under most circumstances. With more luck now available, you have what it takes to get ahead and can invent new ways of dealing with tedious routines. Friends could be supportive now.

⑧ *December*

2009

1 TUESDAY   *Moon Age Day 14   Moon Sign Taurus*

The start of a new month coincides with the lunar high, so you can start December with a real flourish. You can make the most of increased physical energy and a determination to succeed that might surprise you and positively shock colleagues or friends. Don't get hung up on details, because it's the big picture that matters now.

2 WEDNESDAY   *Moon Age Day 15   Moon Sign Gemini*

You have scope to get material matters going very much your way and to fit any amount of work into a day that favours you from the start. Look out for gains coming from a partner's money and from an increased sense of purpose on your part. It just seems that everything falls into place when you need it the most, but it's skill and not luck.

3 THURSDAY   *Moon Age Day 16   Moon Sign Gemini*

Mental effort is favoured at this time, and you can use it to solve puzzles that fox those around you. You have potential to attract a good deal of adulation, sometimes from fairly unexpected directions. At the same time there may be irrevocable decisions to be taken, and some of these will need careful thought.

4 FRIDAY   *Moon Age Day 17   Moon Sign Cancer*

This ought to be a pretty good day for general communication but it could feel slightly less secure on the financial front. You may not be as naturally careful as would usually be the case, and mistakes can be made as a result. It's time to capitalise on something you hear on the grapevine that could turn out to be highly significant.

5 SATURDAY
Moon Age Day 18   Moon Sign Cancer

Look towards a period that is good for re-evaluating your opinions. Not everything in life is the same as it once was, and that can mean having to part with some regular actions or even possessions that are no longer of any use to you. Habit for its own sake is only going to get in the way, even if you are over-nostalgic in some respects.

6 SUNDAY
Moon Age Day 19   Moon Sign Leo

From a social point of view you can make this a day filled with interest and potential. For the first time you may be realising that Christmas is just around the corner, so you might decide to spend at least part of today wrestling with strings of lights or planning lists of presents. Organisation is the key to happiness at the moment.

7 MONDAY
Moon Age Day 20   Moon Sign Leo

There is much to be said for working things through carefully with your partner, especially on the home front. It's possible that you are not yet as organised for Christmas as you would wish to be and the time is approaching quickly. Decisions may also have to be made at work, in response to the behaviour of colleagues.

8 TUESDAY
Moon Age Day 21   Moon Sign Virgo

You have what it takes to get yourself noticed and to put yourself in the spotlight – even when you would prefer not to be. If nothing else all this attention can do your ego the power of good and you shouldn't have too much trouble coming up with the goods when it matters the most. Concentration is vital at work.

9 WEDNESDAY
Moon Age Day 22   Moon Sign Virgo

Trends assist you to gain plenty of support, and to show a great deal of care and concern for others yourself. Make the most of a warm and considerate sort of day all round, with some special highlights later on. An ideal time for making contact with those who live at a distance.

10 THURSDAY
Moon Age Day 23   Moon Sign Libra

There should be no lack of things to do at this stage of the week, and it may be difficult to attract support from those around. You are inclined to be rather more outspoken than might sometimes be the case but would be wise to temper your attitude in order to accommodate those of a timid nature.

11 FRIDAY
Moon Age Day 24   Moon Sign Libra

It seems as though the sort of emotional support you are looking for may be thin on the ground. At the moment the Moon occupies your solar twelfth house and this alone can indicate isolation. In few days you can use positive trends to sweep away any sort of doubt and for the moment you simply need to understand yourself.

12 SATURDAY
Moon Age Day 25   Moon Sign Libra

It may be more difficult than normal to explain yourself to others. Nevertheless it will be worth the effort because you will only get the support and help you need when other people are conversant with your thinking. Rather than rushing your fences today, be prepared to take time out to weigh up the pros and cons of almost any situation.

13 SUNDAY
Moon Age Day 26   Moon Sign Scorpio

Getting ahead might be difficult today, which is why if you are wise you may decide not to try. Instead of knocking your head against a brick wall, why not watch and wait for a couple of days? For Taureans who are not at work today there should be a chance to put your feet up and to let others take the strain.

14 MONDAY
Moon Age Day 27   Moon Sign Scorpio

Making extreme decisions is not to be advised and neither is gambling of almost any sort. Like a cat after a bird your best approach is to move very slowly and to leave the final spring until later. The lunar low this month has been fairly potent, so don't be surprised if you feel slightly exhausted and not really up for life's challenges.

15 TUESDAY *Moon Age Day 28 Moon Sign Sagittarius*

You have what it takes to get back to normal now and to see progress accelerating your life. With Christmas just around the corner there are decisions to be made and the social whirl may already be starting. Energy levels are rising, helping you to meet almost any challenge that life puts before you.

16 WEDNESDAY *Moon Age Day 0 Moon Sign Sagittarius*

A day to get things on course when it comes to practical matters and all arrangements. It is possible to get in touch with powerful emotions at the moment and to confront issues you have been putting to the back of your mind in recent days. In social settings you have scope to demonstrate just how funny you are capable of being.

17 THURSDAY *Moon Age Day 1 Moon Sign Capricorn*

A romance or love affair at this time could prove to be all-consuming and people you meet at the moment may have a lasting emotional impact on your life. If jobs today seem to take twice as long as usual, that might be because you insist on getting every nuance and detail right. Others may laugh at your attitude.

18 FRIDAY *Moon Age Day 2 Moon Sign Capricorn*

There are gains to be made if you opt for wide-open spaces and for alterations in your daily routines. Comfort and security can take something of a back seat as you set out to explore the world with eyes wide open and a sense of wonder in your heart. Bringing yourself back to the essentials of life probably won't be easy at any time today.

19 SATURDAY *Moon Age Day 3 Moon Sign Capricorn*

Your energies can now be put to good use, especially when you are in the company of people you know are in a position to give you a helping hand. Your strength lies in your good ideas, and you could be making discoveries that will have a positive bearing on your life in the weeks ahead. The social scene is highlighted now.

20 SUNDAY   *Moon Age Day 4   Moon Sign Aquarius*

Close twosomes have a positive part to play at the moment and you are capable of finding just the right words to make your partner feel wanted and secure. The same is true in reverse, because expressions of love can bring a sense of warmth into your day and make it rather special. Beware of getting too tied down with pointless routines just now.

21 MONDAY   *Moon Age Day 5   Moon Sign Aquarius*

Tensions at home can come from trying to get too much done in too short a period of time. Maybe you are worrying a lot, or fretting about the Christmas holidays. Things that don't get sorted out to your exacting standards will still come and go, and then you will wonder why you worried at all!

22 TUESDAY   *Moon Age Day 6   Moon Sign Pisces*

Trends highlight your considerable charm, and you can use this to attract a great deal of positive attention from others. With the big day getting very close you will want to put a finishing touch to certain plans, but might be hampered by factors beyond your own control. Alternative strategies may be called for now.

23 WEDNESDAY   *Moon Age Day 7   Moon Sign Pisces*

It seems as though you will get on better today if you do your own thing, rather than catering for everyone else. That doesn't mean you are being selfish. Not everyone has your staying power or your ability to work quickly through potential problems. By tomorrow you can afford to be feeling more settled and secure.

24 THURSDAY   *Moon Age Day 8   Moon Sign Pisces*

Today is good for all intimate matters, and that is basically because Venus still occupies your solar eighth house. The time is right for decisions regarding a romantic matter, and though this might not suit everyone it puts your mind at rest. Be prepared to reach out to help friends because one or two of them would welcome your input.

25 FRIDAY
Moon Age Day 9   Moon Sign Aries

Christmas Day might not start out quite as hectic as you have been expecting. Things seem to fall into place on their own and you can get others to pitch in and lend a hand. Solutions can be found to those typical sort of problems – like did we buy batteries for that, and if so where are they? All in all you can make this a day to remember.

26 SATURDAY
Moon Age Day 10   Moon Sign Aries

Social trends are now in the ascendant, and even if you still don't have quite the level of get up and go that is possible tomorrow, you can afford to mix and mingle. There are moments when a little solitude will seem to be very appealing, and time spent with your partner will be the most valuable of all.

27 SUNDAY
Moon Age Day 11   Moon Sign Taurus

This has potential to be the most positive period of the entire Christmas week. The Moon returns to your zodiac sign and brings with it greater energy and a determination to be involved in everything. You can afford to back your hunches to the hilt and that will prove to be especially useful if you happen to be working at this time.

28 MONDAY
Moon Age Day 12   Moon Sign Taurus

You should now be feeling as if your luck is really in. All sorts of bonuses are on offer, and you have the ability to be in the place where the action is. Getting on well with almost everyone is a piece of cake right now, and this could be the best time of all to ask someone for a favour. Why not? The worst they can do is to say no.

29 TUESDAY
Moon Age Day 13   Moon Sign Taurus

You may well be feeling now as if you want to overdo everything and to live your life in a grand style. The lunar high also assists you to persuade others to join in with your ideas. The need for luxury is strong and it's worth grasping any opportunity to spoil yourself. Your creative potential is also favoured.

30 WEDNESDAY *Moon Age Day 14   Moon Sign Gemini*

You can expand your experience base today by doing something completely different. After all, a new year lies just around the corner and that's a time when alternative experiences are most opportune. Some of you may be feeling as if the time is right to get back to normal life but for the next day or two you need to curb your impatience.

31 THURSDAY *Moon Age Day 15   Moon Sign Gemini*

All communication matters are positively highlighted today. The Moon is in your solar third house and that helps you to get into a perfect state of mind for those New Year parties. Whatever you decide to do with yourself this evening, you can get others to fall in line and do everything they can to make you happy.

RISING SIGNS FOR TAURUS

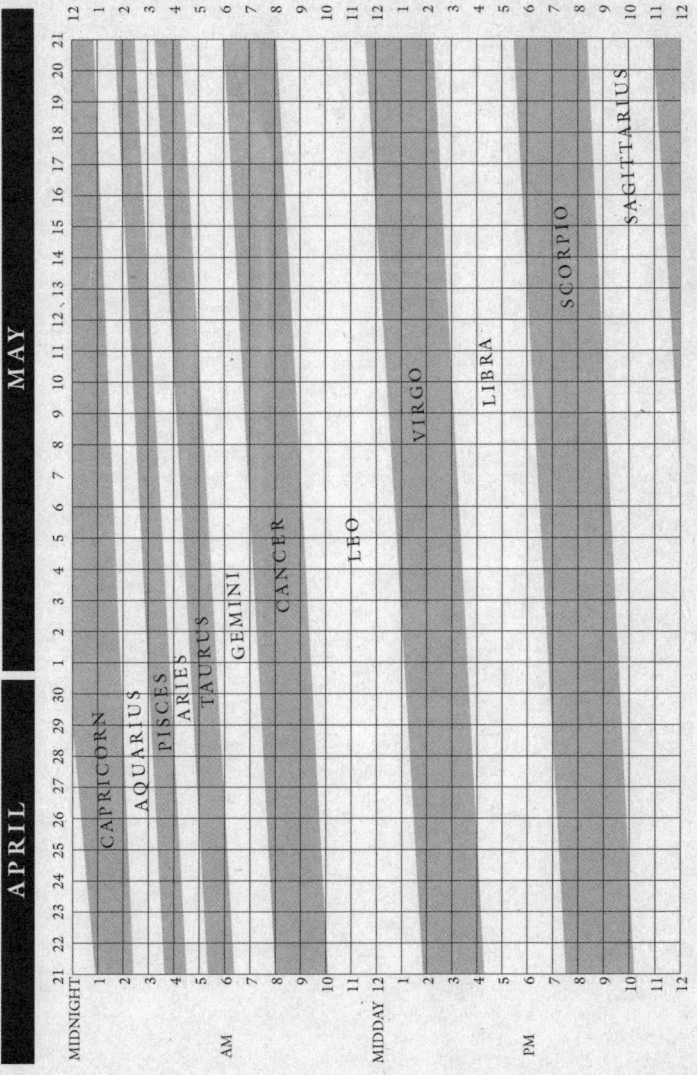

THE ZODIAC, PLANETS AND CORRESPONDENCES

The Earth revolves around the Sun once every calendar year, so when viewed from Earth the Sun appears in a different part of the sky as the year progresses. In astrology, these parts of the sky are divided into the signs of the zodiac and this means that the signs are organised in a circle. The circle begins with Aries and ends with Pisces.

Taking the zodiac sign as a starting point, astrologers then work with all the positions of planets, stars and many other factors to calculate horoscopes and birth charts and tell us what the stars have in store for us.

The table below shows the planets and Elements for each of the signs of the zodiac. Each sign belongs to one of the four Elements: Fire, Air, Earth or Water. Fire signs are creative and enthusiastic; Air signs are mentally active and thoughtful; Earth signs are constructive and practical; Water signs are emotional and have strong feelings.

It also shows the metals and gemstones associated with, or corresponding with, each sign. The correspondence is made when a metal or stone possesses properties that are held in common with a particular sign of the zodiac.

Finally, the table shows the opposite of each star sign – this is the opposite sign in the astrological circle.

Placed	Sign	Symbol	Element	Planet	Metal	Stone	Opposite
1	Aries	Ram	Fire	Mars	Iron	Bloodstone	Libra
2	Taurus	Bull	Earth	Venus	Copper	Sapphire	Scorpio
3	Gemini	Twins	Air	Mercury	Mercury	Tiger's Eye	Sagittarius
4	Cancer	Crab	Water	Moon	Silver	Pearl	Capricorn
5	Leo	Lion	Fire	Sun	Gold	Ruby	Aquarius
6	Virgo	Maiden	Earth	Mercury	Mercury	Sardonyx	Pisces
7	Libra	Scales	Air	Venus	Copper	Sapphire	Aries
8	Scorpio	Scorpion	Water	Pluto	Plutonium	Jasper	Taurus
9	Sagittarius	Archer	Fire	Jupiter	Tin	Topaz	Gemini
10	Capricorn	Goat	Earth	Saturn	Lead	Black Onyx	Cancer
11	Aquarius	Waterbearer	Air	Uranus	Uranium	Amethyst	Leo
12	Pisces	Fishes	Water	Neptune	Tin	Moonstone	Virgo